THE 7TH PANZER DIVISION
IN FRANCE AND RUSSIA
ROMMEL'S GHOST DIVISION

BY
DR. RUSSEL H. S. STOLFI

Pen & Sword
MILITARY

This edition first published in Great Britain in 2014
and re-print in 2015 by
PEN & SWORD MILITARY
An imprint of
Pen & Sword Books Ltd
47 Church Street
Barnsley, South Yorkshire
S70 2AS

Copyright © Coda Books Ltd, 2014, 2015

ISBN 978 1 78346 246 9

A CIP catalogue record for this book
is available from the British Library

Printed and bound in England
By CPI Group (UK) Ltd, Croydon, CR0 4YY

Pen & Sword Books Ltd incorporates the Imprints of Aviation, Atlas,
Family History, Fiction, Maritime, Military, Discovery, Politics, History,
Archaeology, Select, Wharncliffe Local History, Wharncliffe True Crime,
Military Classics, Wharncliffe Transport, Leo Cooper, The Praetorian Press,
Remember When, Seaforth Publishing and Frontline Publishing

For a complete list of Pen & Sword titles please contact
PEN & SWORD BOOKS LIMITED
47 Church Street, Barnsley, South Yorkshire, S70 2AS, England
E-mail: enquiries@pen-and-sword.co.uk
Website: www.pen-and-sword.co.uk

Table of Contents

Chapters

Figures

Maps

Chapter 1

The 7th Panzer Division in the French Campaign, May 1940

World War II analysts often refer to the German campaign against France as the Six Week's War. They do this to highlight the extraordinary speed with which the Germans achieved victory in a campaign that began on 10 May 1940 and did not involve much fighting beyond 17 June 1940 - the day on which France's Marshal Henri-Philippe Petain asked the Germans for an armistice. To grasp the scope of the German achievement in France, the "Six Weeks War" should perhaps be called the "Five Weeks War," or even the "Four Days War." The Germans took approximately five days to regroup for the attack across the Somme, so actual combat took place over a period of only about five weeks. Furthermore, the Germans achieved the decisive turning point in the campaign when they forced crossings of the Meuse (Maas) River at several points on 13 May 1940 *only four days* into the battle. The Germans, in effect, won the Battle of France in four days because of the crossing of the river barrier combined with the immediate exploitation of the crossing by the swift advances of the 7th Panzer Division and others deep into the Allied rear.

The German 7th Panzer Division (hereafter referred to as 7.Pz.D.)[1], operating under the direction of the XVth Panzer Corps (XV.A.K. (mot.)), advanced with greater effect arguably, than any other German division in the West. There were other fine divisions. The German I.Pz.D., lying

---

1. See Figure 1 for unit abbreviations used in this study. Note that in German, 7., is equivalent to English, 7th. In German, the decimal point represents the ordinal numbers (i.e., those which indicate the order in which things come) and replaces the "th" and "rd" and "st" used in English. The system is simpler and will be used throughout to give a flavor for the German style of expression.

farther south in XIX.A.K. (mot), for example, advanced with similar urgency and effect. But the 7.Pz.D. not only achieved more but it fought with an offensive skill unexcelled in modern times. The 7.Pz.D. approach to warfighting was truly remarkable and holds lessons for the Marine Corps and other western ground combat forces today. Just what were the accomplishments of 7.Pz.D? And what was the spirit and style of command that characterized this division as it made some of the most spectacular advances in modern times?

Perhaps the search for answers should begin with Erwin Rommel. *Generalmajor* (Brigadier General) Erwin Rommel, fresh from his assignment as commander of the *Fuhrer Begleiter Bataillon* (*Fuhrer Escort Battalion*), became the commander of 7.Pz.D. on 12 February 1940 in time to put a special stamp on the division associated with his name.

Even today Rommel tends to overshadow 7.Pz.D. and its achievements during the Battle of France. Time and again, Rommel devised the push forward that had a campaign-level impact on the western offensive: the crossing of the Meuse, the push through the French border fortifications, the successful blunting of the Allied counterattack at Arras, the penetration of the Somme River defenses in a single day. Rommel simply would suffer no tactical impasse. When the northern path of attack over the Meuse 800m south of Houx began to falter in the face of heavy fire, Rommel went personally to the spot and ordered his tanks into the open on the banks of the crossing site so that they could support the attack with direct fire. The attack was successful. On the next morning when the bridgehead was threatened by strong French tank attacks, Rommel - again personally on the spot - ordered his troops to fire their light-signalling pistols at the tanks coming through the morning mist; he told the troops that the French tanks would veer off in the surprise and uncertainty of the situation. They did. Rommel's operational and tactical instincts would ultimately place him in the category of

English	German	German Abbreviation
7th Armored Division	7.Panzer-Division	7.Pz.Div. or 7.Pz.D.
The Main Maneuver Elements:		
25th Armored Regiment	Panzer-Regiment 25	Pz.Rgt. 25 or Pz.R. 25
7th Motorized Rifle Regiment	Schutzen Regiment 7	S.R. 7
6th Motorized Rifle Regiment	Schutzen Regiment 6	S.R. 6
37th Armored Reconnaissance Detachment	Panzer Aufklarungs-Abteilung 37	Pz.A.A. 37
7th Motorcycle Battalion	Kradschutzen-Bataillon 7	
The Main Combat Support Elements:		
78th Artillery Regiment	Artillerie-Regiment 78	A.R. 78
58th Pioneer Battalion	Pionier-Bataillon 58	Pi. 58
42nd Antitank Detachment	Panzerjager-Abteilung 42	Pz.Vg. 42
59th Light Anti-aircraft Detachment	Leichte Flak Abteilung 59	Fla. 59

Figure 1. Abbreviations Used for 7th Panzer Division and its Organic Units.

military genius. But the quality and achievements of the 7.Pz.D. went far beyond one man.

The division had qualities in its subordinate commanders, staff officers, combat soldiers and their weapons and equipment that ensured this Panzer division and others like it would have been formidable in war with or without Rommel. The 7.Pz.D. had a common approach to warfighting that gave them great speed, flexibility and a tremendous talent for communicating much in few words - and sometimes in no words at all. Later in WWII, 7.Pz.D., took this approach to war to Russia and under a new commander, *Generalmajor* von Funck (commander of 5.Pz.R, 5.Pz.D. in France), 7.Pz.D. achieved results even more impressive than those in France.

• • • • •

But Russia lay in the distance, France was the immediate challenge. As usual, 7.Pz.D. moved quickly. Led by Rommel, as part of the XV.A.K. (mot.), 7.Pz.D. advanced at 0530 on 10 May 1940 into the undefended but "strong and deep border obstacles"[2] of the hilly and forested terrain of the Belgian Ardennes south of the old city of Aachen (Aix-la-Chapelle). Rommel's mission - and that of the whole XV.A.K. (mot.) - was to guard the right flank of the German *Schwerpunkt*[3], Panzer Group Kleist, to the South. The danger was of an Allied attack from the north using forces already massed in Belgium. Rommel pushed the division so hard that it quickly outdistanced the neighboring 5.Pz.D. to the north and, not too surprisingly, the neighboring 32.1.D. (Infantry Division) to the south. Rommel employed *Kradschutzen Bataillon* 7 (K.7, or Motorcycle Battalion 7) and *Panzer Aufklarungs Abteilung* 37, (Pz.A.A.37, or Armored Reconnaissance Detachment 37, a battalion-strength organization) as the lead elements of the advance. In both France (1940) and Russia (1941)[4], the commanding generals of 7.Pz.D. would use K.7 and Pz.A.A.37 as the lead elements. Rommel and Funck used these mobile ground elements extensively for reconnaissance, often breaking them up into small elements and sending them off in multiple directions to find out what was going

---

2. See in, *7.Pa.D., Ia, Kurzberichte, 10.5.40*, U.S., Archives, German Records, Division, T-315, Roll 401, Fr. 000624.

3. Literally, heavy point. The Germans used the term figuratively to denote the crucial focus in an attack *or* on the defensive. The term is associated both with a physical area and associated formation of troops, e.g., in the first stage of the French Campaign, the *Schwerpunkt* was *with* Panzer Group Kleist *through* Sedan *to* the coast of the English Channel.

4. The author will use the term, Russia, to describe the operating area in the east interchangeably with Soviet Union because of the persistent German use of the term *Russland* in describing the area.

on. Most often, both generals used these elements in tandem as the advanced detachments along the main axis of the division's advance.

On the first day of the attack against France, Major V. Steinkeller led K7 as the advanced element of the entire division in the drive through the Ardennes. The battalion was a lightly armed, mobile force organized as follows:

K.7.: German Ultra-Mobile Advanced Combat Detachment and Reconnaissance Element of May 1940.[5]

H.Q. Detachment: Mounted largely on motorcycles.

Weapons Detachment: 6 80mm mortars, 3 37mm AT guns.

Two Motorcycle Companies: each w/3 50mm mortars, 4 hvy mgs, 18 lt mgs.

The Germans used K.7 to advance into the Ardennes through the light Belgian screening forces. Although nimble and lightly armed, K.7 was basically a combat (as opposed to reconnaissance) force. K7 was often reinforced by other elements that gave it impressive strength, e.g., a tank company, antitank platoon, artillery battery, pioneer platoon, Flak (antiaircraft) battery, or *Schutzen* (motorized infantry) company. On the first day of the attack, 10 May 40, K.7 led the division toward the crossing of the Ourthe River, the major obstacle on the way to the Meuse.

The next morning on 11 May 40, led by K7 and Pz.A.A.37 moving along separate axes, 7.Pz.D. crossed the Ourthe River through a ford at Beffe, near Marcount and across a bridge captured intact near La Roche en Ardenne. K.7 reinforced by 6./A.R.78, (6th Battery, Artillery Regiment 78, the regiment organic to 7.Pz.D.) comprising four 105mm

---

5.   See in H. Scheibert, *Die Gespenster-Division, Eine Deutsche Panzer-Division (7.) im Zweiten Weltkrieg* (Dorheim, no date), p. 24.

truck towed howitzers, engaged a "strong French mechanized unit with tanks and artillery at its disposal"[6] near the major road junction at Marche. This was on the direct route to Dinant on the Meuse now only about 35 km distant by road. As this action developed, PzAA.37, advancing north of the motorcyclists took the town of Marche itself. Since the morning of the previous day, 10 May 40, 7.Pz.D. had traversed about 90 km road distance through the Ardennes. The division had set a rapid pace; the First General Staff Officer (referred to hereafter as "Ia") of the division noted laconically in the short history of the campaign that during the advance on 11 May 40, "there was not contact with either of the neighboring units,"[7] 5.Pz.D. to the north and 32.1.D to the south. Casualties were light: 3 KIA, 7 WIA, and 3 MIA. The division awarded one E.K. I to Lieutenant Schrock of Pz.A.A.37. Rommel and 7.Pz.D. were moving fast, looking neither left nor right nor over their shoulders, and keeping the screening and delaying forces of the enemy off balance.

In spite of the remarkable advance of the forward detachments of 7.Pz.D., the French massed strong forces blocking the way to Dinant (on the Meuse) during the late afternoon and evening of 11 May 40. Without hesitation, Rommel committed Pz.R.25 (Panzer Regiment 25) and S.R. 7 (Motorized Infantry Regiment 7) to an attack that opened at 0700 12 May 40. *Oberst* (Colonel) Rothenburg with Pz.R. 25 broke through the French defenders at 1000 and pushed on west of Leignon toward Dinant only 27 km distant. 7.Pz.Div. was advancing even faster than the rest of the speeding German army. The division had advanced so quickly that the corps commander, *General* Hoth, ordered 7.Pz.D. to take command of the strong *Vorausabteilung* (advanced detachment) of the neighboring 5.Pz.D. The mass of 5.Pz.D. lay well behind 7.Pz.D.

At 1645 on 12 May, the tank company of *Hauptmann* (Captain)

---

6. See, *7.Pz.D., Ia, Kurzberichte, 11.5.40*, U.S., Archives, German Records, Division, T-315, Roll 401, Fr. 000625.

7. Ibid.

Steffen, reinforced by part of I./S.R.7 (1st Battalion, 7th Motorized Infantry Regiment), reached the Meuse at Dinant. In contrast, farther south in the campaign level *Schwerpunkt* of Panzer Group Kleist, the armored troops of *General der Panzertruppe* Heinz Guderian's XIXA.K. (mot.) did not reach the Meuse until several hours later, 2300 on the evening of 12 May 40, at Sedan.[8] When Kleist and Guderian ordered their main attack to begin at 1600 13 May 40, they had the continuous support of the *Schwerpunkt* ground attack aircraft of the Luftwaffe - virtually all of the Stukas available in the west, screened and defended as appropriate by the German fighter force. Rommel to the north could depend on only modest air support and his own artillery, tank cannons, and Flak weapons. Nevertheless, Rommel organized an attack - not for 1600 - but for first light on 13 May 40. (See Map 1.)

7.Pz.D. pushed its first elements across the Meuse at 0430 and gained by force two secure bridgeheads after several hours of hard combat. K.7 and S.R. 6 reinforced by pioneers and *Pak* (antitank guns)[9] seized the northern lodgement near Houx as S.R.7, reinforced by pioneers, seized the southern bridgehead near Dinant. The defending French troops launched very strong counterattacks supported by tanks and artillery in the afternoon and early evening against the German motorcyclists of K.7 and the riflemen of S.R.6. As darkness fell, the Germans began to ferry across tanks and armored reconnaissance vehicles. It had been a day of severe combat; the division lost 60 KIA, 122 WIA, and 6 MIA, and awarded 16 E.K. I, those of *Oberleutnant* Topfer of S.R.7 and *Leutnant* Neubrand of K.7 mentioned as having been won under particularly significant tactical circumstances.

The German use of speed as a weapon was illustrated by their use of the hours of darkness. Rommel's presence, leadership and

---

8. See in, Hermann Balck, *Ordnung im Chaos, Erinnerungen 1893-1948* (Osnabruck, 1980) - p. 269, where the author notes the leading troops of the leading division (1.Pz.D.) of *Pz. Gr.* Kleist reaching the Meuse at 2300, 12.5.40. Balck commanded S.R.1 of I.Pz.D.

9. *Pak* or *Panzerabwehrkanone* or antitank cannon. The word has not become household in English as is the case with Flak (anti-aircraft fire) and will be italicized in the study.

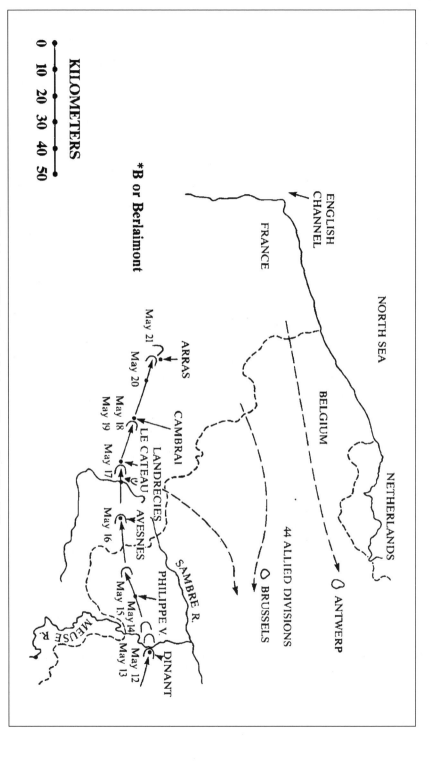

Map 1. Advance of 7.Pz.D. Through Belgium and France, (12-21 May 1941).

influence had propelled 7.Pz.D throughout the southern crossing near Dinant. Now, with the sun having set, was the time to reform and rest after the difficult crossing. Common sense seemed to demand a break in the offense. Instead, Rommel continued the attack. During the early hours of darkness "on the basis of the order from XV.A.K. (mot.),"[10] he launched S.R.7 out of the southern enclave in an advance against Onhaye, a village 5 km west of the crossing site near Dinant. The soldiers of 7.Pz.D. had been on the move and engaged in heavy combat all day 12 May 40 and then without rest preparing for a crossing of the Meuse that began at 0430 on 13 May. Fighting continuously on 13 May, the division must have been a candidate for physical and psychological exhaustion by darkness on that day. Furthermore, the division had been constantly on the move since 0530 on 10 May 1940 in its challenging traverse of the Ardennes. Yet Hoth ordered a night advance west out of the still coalescing bridgeheads; Rommel almost certainly would have followed the same course of action without any prompting from Corps headquarters. What kind of thinking drove Hoth and Rommel at this stage of the offensive in the west? Only a fundamental understanding of the power unleashed by speed and relentlessness.

7.Pz.D. had lost contact the previous day (12 May 40) with *both* of its neighbors. The Ia of the division noted, for example, that on 12 May the whereabouts of the mass of 5.Pz.D. was unknown and that no connection existed with 32.I.D. on the left. Things did not improve much on 13 May because only about two or three companies of 5.Pz.D. succeeded in forcing a crossing of the Meuse near Houx to the north of 7.Pz.D. 32.I.D. only drew near the Meuse 10 km south and slightly west of Dinant. Rommel advanced with S.R.7 reinforced by *"Panzerjager"* probably referring to a significant part of *Panzerjager-Abteilung* 42, the division's battalion-level Antitank Detachment (hereinafter referred to as Pz.Jg.42).

---

10. 7.Pz.D., Ia, Kurzberichte, Supra.

Rommel advanced with exhausted troops, over unfamiliar terrain, in full darkness, and with no friendly forces on either flank. Speed was both his weapon and his protection. Suddenly trouble developed. The lead regiment, S.R.7, advanced to the eastern edge of Onhaye before it sent out a radio call just before dawn that it had been surrounded *(eingeschlossen)* by the French around Onhaye. This apparently signaled a dramatic change in fortune for the Germans and the collapse of optimistic expectations for a breakthrough. Rommel gathered up all the tanks and armored reconnaissance vehicles that had been ferried across the Meuse, put himself at their head, and personally rushed to the assistance of S.R.7. Rommel discovered that the regiment had radioed not *eingeschlossen* (surrounded) but *eingetroffen* (struck), or that it has been hit hard by what turned out to be the first of several French tank attacks around Onhaye.[11] One must respect Clausewitz for his comments on war as friction and uncertainty. It is worth considering also, whether an American division commander today would gather up and move instantly at the head of a column of armored vehicles? Division command posts in today's western ground forces have tended to become small cities with large bureaucracies. The benefits of this approach are hard to see; the benefits of Rommel's approach are compelling. At daybreak early on 14 May 1940, S.R.7 threw back several French tank attacks with the assistance of the tanks brought forward by Rommel. Rommel kept 7.Pz.D. advancing by leading from the front. The method was not without its drawbacks. Just west of Onhaye, under *direct fire* from two batteries of French 75 mm field guns and some *Pak*, Rommel's tank received a direct hit and he was lightly wounded.

At 0900 14 May 40, Hoth (in a quick move of his own) placed all of the units belonging to 5.Pz.D west of the river under the commander of 7.Pz.D.. For the remainder of the day, with Pz.R.25, S.R.7, and S.R.6, i.e., the mass of the mission, now across the river, all under Rommel's

---

11. See in, *7.Pz.D., Ia, Kriegsberichte, 14.5.40*, U.S., Archives, German Records, Divisions, T-315, Roll 401, Fr. 000686.

command, the Germans fought off continuous French attacks in the area around and to the north of Onhaye.

The Stuka (Junkers 87 B-I and similar B-variants) aircraft proved to be effective on this day in breaking up strong attacks from the west by French mechanized forces. Rommel and 7.Pz.D. went through another day of high intensity combat and the additional strain of having to develop the crossings over the Meuse River. The practical question arises: what kept the German combat soldiers awake? Yet at 1930 on 14 May 40, 7.Pz.D., which had mastered the French counterattacks, advanced with the intention of taking Morville, 7 km west of Onhaye. Pz.R.25 under *Oberst* Rothenburg led the advance and Rommel stationed himself personally with the regiment to ensure continued movement in the face of uncertainty, danger, fear, and the heavy fatigue of the troops. Rommel, Rothenburg, and the tank regiment seized Morville at 2230 in the face of tough resistance by the French. 7.Pz.D. completed another day of continuous lighting and movement in which it had taken casualties of 51 KIA and 158 WIA and awarded 19 E.K. I.

The division was now 12 km west of the Meuse at about midnight on 14 May 40 but the heavy casualties of the last two days of combat showed that it had not broken through the French defenders. The division had led the combat march through the Ardennes, had been the leader across the Meuse, and would be the division first to break away from the defensive zone along the Meuse. The division used K7 and Pz.A.A.37 as the leading elements in the fluid situation in the Ardennes pushing them along two axes of advance when the road system allowed, or cross-country when forced by Belgian and French resistance. The "motorcyclists" and the "armored car soldiers" seem to have given the commanding generals of 7.Pz.D. the capability to move out more quickly from a standing start than would have been possible with tanks and motorized infantry.

The Ia of the division commented in his report of the crossing, that by the onset of darkness, the first tanks and armored reconnaissance vehicles had begun to be ferried across the river. Given the pressure on the bridgeheads by evening of 13 May 40, the Germans, perhaps, should have been more concerned with Flak and antitank guns to defend their precarious hold. The division decided, to the contrary, to use precious ferry space to bring over armored reconnaissance vehicles armed with 20 mm cannon, largely useless in defense against the French tanks of the day, but vital to the division commander in exploiting an advance out of the lodgements. Again and again Rommel and his staff emphasized continuing the attack rather than consolidating hard won gains.

Rommel by this time had originated a unique system of directing the division units by means of what he called the *"Stosslinie der Division"*[12] (thrust line of the division). As appropriate, in written orders or radio and phone messages, the division Ia designated the thrust line for given time periods and directed the maneuver of subordinate units of the divisions along it. The Ia always designated the thrust line in terms of a beginning point and an ending point clearly identifiable on the 1:100,000 or 1:300,000 maps being used to conduct operations. On some occasions the thrust line would include a single turning point, i.e., a thrust line did not ordinarily have but might have a single angle in it. A thrust line would most often begin with zero and always be marked at one-kilometer intervals for its entire length. The units of 7.Pz.D. would talk to one another in terms of locations along this line, for example, "14 right 1 km," meaning 14 km along the line and right 1.5 km. Rommel had created a psychological masterpiece by moving the division in terms of an inspiring great arrow on the map instead of soulless map coordinates. The system was also flexible, simple, and secure, e.g., towns, road junctions, and other geographical points were rarely mentioned in orders or messages directing the movements of the division. (See Figure 2, in appendix, for an example of a thrust line.)

---

12.   See for example, *7. Panzer-Division; Ia, Gefechts-und Erfahrungsberichte Abschrift, Betr; Funkbetrieb, Div. St. Qu., den 11.6 40*, U.S. Archives, German Records, Divisions, T-315, Roll 436, Fr. 000736.

German commanders and staff officers worded their messages in a manner that gives valuable clues to their style in conducting mobile operations. The messages tended to be compact and starkly brief. They reflected a special kind of self confidence and initiative on the part of the senders. Note the following exchange early in the campaign (See Figures 3, 4, 5, 6, in appendix, for the messages themselves):

MESSAGE			
Date	Time	From-To	Message Wording
13.5	0420	5.Pz.D. to 7.Pz.D.	*Angriff 0430* (Our attack is going in at 0430)[13]
13.5	0550	7.Pz.D. to S.R. 7	*We Lage?* (How are you doing?)[14]

MESSAGE			
Date	Time	From-To	Message Wording
13.5	0640	S.R.7 to T.Pz.D.	*0600 S.R.7 Fluss Maas uberschritten* (7th Motorized Infantry Regiment crossed the Maas River at 0600).[15]
13.5	0730	7.Pz.D. to Pz.A.A.37	*Gefangene zur Division* (Prisoners to the division).[16]

German officers penned these messages during the tense hours of the assault crossing of the Meuse. The messages show a remarkably stark but also streamlined style. They also show that the officers

---

13. *7Pz.D., Ia, Anlagen zum kriegstagebuch, Funkspruch Nr. 2A*, 13.5.40, U.S., Archives, German Records, T-315, Roll 402 Fr. 000014.

14. Ibid., Nr. 66, Fr. 000017.

15. *7.Pz.D., Ia, Anlagen zum Kriegstagebuch, Meldung Nr. 104*, U.S. Archives, German Records, Divisions, T-315, Roll 402, Fr. 000025.

16. *7.Pz.D., Ia, Anlagen zum Kriegstagebuch, Funkspruch Nr. 13*, U.S. Archives, German Records, Division, T-315, Roll 402, Fr. 000025.

writing them shared a common, no-nonsense operational language. The following message illustrates the direct style of the Germans in which unit commanders addressed themselves directly to the division commander, in this case Major Erdmann speaking directly to "the general." (See also Figure 7. in appendix):

MESSAGE			
Date	Time	From-To	Message Wording
13.5	0645	Pz.A.A-37 (Major Erdmann) to The General	The message is obscured by fire damage. It begins though by developing the situation of Pz.A.A.37 around 0600 13.5.40.

German divisions had small operations and quartermaster (logistics) staffs. The operations staff was particularly small in numbers and light in rank. As formally organized, 7.Pz.D. had no assistant division commander and no executive officer in any component element. The division had no chief of staff but rather a 1st general staff officer (operations) (Ia), *Major, i.G.* (*Major im Generalstab*, or Major of the General Staff) Heidkamper, who ran the internal affairs of the division, coordinated the parts, and maintained contact with neighboring units to left and right and the next higher headquarters. Young as he was, he was also the first advisor to the commanding general on the combat operations of the division. He did his job largely with the assistance of the intelligence officer (Ic), *Major Ziegler* (not a general staff officer) and the division quartermaster *Hauptmann i.G.* von Metzsch. These junior officers dominated the division Operations Staff and Quartermaster Detachment. *Major i.G.* Heidkamper had a close and confident relationship with the commanding general based not on rank but on his undoubted competence as a general staff officer. The self confidence and initiative are illustrated by the following message (See also Figure 8. in appendix):[17]

17. *7.Pz.D., Ia, Anlagen zum Kriegstagebuch, Funkspruch Nr. 4*, U.S., Archives, German Records, Divisions, T-315, Roll 402-Fr. 000032.

MESSAGE			
Date	**Time**	**From-To**	**Message Wording**
13.5	0700	*Fuhrg. Staffel* (Operations Staff) to The General	Wie Luftlage? Sollen wir Jagdfluz erfordern? (How is the air situation? Should we request fighters?)

With his streamlined operations staff and without the massive bureaucracy characteristic of today's division command post and operations staff, the German *Panzer* division commander had a more direct relationship with his commanders and a greater opportunity to lead the division from the front. Rommel was particularly aggressive and placed himself forward not only by natural predilection and the opportunity afforded by his compact operations staff, but also because he had achieved a special insight into the uncertainty, chance, and danger of war. Based on his success in combat in World War I, he seems to have understood that the most effective way to overcome the chaos of war was to personally stay with the offensive *Schwerpunkt* force, maintain the initiative and, thereby reduce the uncertainty of war. The following message illustrates Rommel at the front of various spearhead detachments struggling to break out of the bridgehead:[18]

MESSAGE			
Date	**Time**	**From-To**	**Message Wording**
14.5	0810	*Gen* (General) *to Div. Gt.* (Div. Command Post)	Rommel hilft Bismarck mit Panzern. (Rommel to the assistance of Bismarck (CO, S.R.7) with tanks)

The time is the morning of 14 May 40 and the message shows Rommel personally leading tanks of the newly arriving Pz.R.25 to

---

18. *7.Pz.D., la, Anlagen, zum Kriegstagebuch, Operationsakten, Spruch Nr. 16*, U.S., Archives, German Records, Divisions, T-315, Roll 402, Fr. 000228.

assist the *Schwerpunkt* of the attack with S.R.7 commanded by *Oberst* v. Bismarck in the southern bridgehead. After fierce engagements during the daylight hours in the bridgehead, Rommel energetically ignited a night advance to attempt to achieve the elusive breakthrough. The following messages show Rommel organizing events from the front to keep the division moving:

MESSAGE			
Date	Time	From-To	Message Wording
14.5	c.1900	Rommel w/ Pz.R.25 to 7.Pz.D.	Rommel Wo funfte panzer Div. (Rommel - Where is 5th Panzer Division?)[19]
14.5	1930	Rommel w/Pz.R.25 to 7.Pz.D.	Rommel 1930 Verfolgung mit allem Waffen. (Rommel 1930 - Pursue with all weapons.)[20]

The messages show that Rommel had concentrated the attack of 7.Pz.D. with Pz.R.25 and is in the process of driving it with S.R.7 westward to complete a breakthrough of the Meuse line of defense. In the first message, Rommel expeditiously uses the communications of Pz.R.25 to query the division staff on the location of the neighboring *Panzer* division. In the second message, he dramatically orders through the division operations staff pursuit of the French with all "weapons" (See also Figures 9, 10 & 11, in appendix).

•   •   •   •   •

Rommel and 7.Pz.D. would achieve their greatest success in the French Campaign in the period 15-21 May 40 with the bold advance out of the Meuse bridgehead in Belgium. The division would accelerate

---

19. Ibid. *Skruch Nr.* 120, Fr. 00327.
20. Ibid. *Skruch Nr.* obscured, Fr. 000326.

through Avesnes in France, continue into a deep drive west of Arras (France), and successfully defend against a nerve-wracking British counterblow thereby cutting off approximately 44 Allied divisions in Belgium. After having arrived at Morville 14 km west of Dinant on the Meuse around midnight on 14 May 40, 7.Pz.D. got the first "rest" in the campaign after five days of continuous moving or fighting. Then, at 1000 the next morning, the division attacked "on the order of XV.A.K. (mot.)" in the direction of Avesnes in France. Rommel deployed Pz.R.25 under *Oberst* Rothenburg as the spearhead of the advance and personally accompanied the tanks himself. Rommel ordered PzAA.37, S.R.7, and part of the division artillery to follow the tanks. He also coordinated a Stuka attack against Philippeville 15 km to the west along the route of the attack. Elements of continuity begin to emerge in the German style of advance. Rommel is forward with the most advanced element of the division, which momentarily is the tank "wedge," the pace of the advance is relentless, and the reconnaissance battalion is close behind the tanks that are expected to run into trouble.

Almost immediately, Pz.R.25 met French tanks and in a short gun battle, they hit and disabled *(Abgeschossen)* seven French "heavy tanks."[21] The official German record of the event does not give the model designation of the French tanks but they would almost certainly have been either the 32-ton *Char B-1 bis* or 20-ton *S.O.M.U.A. 35*. These tanks had armor on both hulls and turrets varying from 40mm-60mm making them too heavily armored to be penetrated by either the antitank guns or the tank cannons of 7.Pz.D.. In this extraordinary situation throughout the French Campaign. 7.Pz.D. (and all other divisions of the German army in France) had to depend on hits to the track system, "lucky" impacts against the junction of turret and hull (to jam the turret), and other similar types of impacts to disable these

---

21. *7.Pz.D., Ia, Kurzberichte: Der Kampf im Westen, Mai-Juni 1940*, U.S., Archives, German Records, Divisions, T-315, Roll 401, Fr. 000688.

vehicles. In this uncomfortable situation, the Germans survived largely by flexible employment of the heavy Flak weapons and 105mm artillery howitzers of the division in direct fire against the tanks.

After disabling the French heavy tanks, Pz.R.25, with Rommel personally accompanying it, drove along *Route Nationale 36* to Philippeville about 13 km west of the tank engagement. Rommel and Rothenburg moved boldly and with strong nerves because the French closed in behind them engaging the following Pz.A.A.37 and S.R.7 for several hours in heavy fighting in which the Germans destroyed 12 heavy and 14 light French tanks. Rommel and Pz.R.25 reached Philippeville at 1300 15 May 40 and secured it and the area around it by 1540.

Although Philippeville had been the target for the entire day's advance and Pz.R.25 was isolated from the mass of the division still delayed behind it, Rommel led the tanks farther west. He was quickly halted by strong French resistance organized around numerous machine guns and antitank guns in defensible terrain about 4 km from the city. Requiring infantry and artillery to continue the advance and still isolated from the mass of the division, Rommel personally drove with reinforced Pz.Kp. Schulz (Panzer Company Schulz) back towards Philippeville to bring forward the rest of the division.

Furious fighting developed between 1730-1900 15 May 40 as a result of this move. Pz.Kp.Schulz and the advanced elements of Pz.A.A.37, with which it had linked up, destroyed 13 French tanks and captured intact 20 additional ones. French armor had been all over the roads and fields between Rommel, Pz.R.25 and the rest of the division, but finally had been eliminated.

At 1900, now in a familiar pattern of continuing action and movement into the evening, the division commander brought forward the foremost elements of the mass of the division - specifically, M.G.Btl.8 (Machine

Gun Battalion 8, attached to 7.Pz.D. from corps troops) - in the area just broken through by the tanks of Pz.R.25 around Senzeille 6 km west of Philippeville. Rommel sited M.G.Btl.8 in defensive positions in support of the tanks of Pz.R.25. He closed up the division in preparation for a continuation of the advance through the fortifications of the French extension of the Maginot Line along the French-Belgian border. 7.Pz.D. had passed through another day of heavy combat with 15 men killed and 56 wounded. The division had taken 450 prisoners and destroyed or captured 75 French tanks. The division had left the rest of the German army far behind on this day; 5.Pz.D. was engaged in a tank battle near the Meuse at Flavion approximately 25 km to the rear of the 7.Pz.D. units west of Senzeille. Rommel and his operations staff on 15 May[22] had no contact with and no longer even knew the whereabouts of 32.1. D. on their left. Rommel's boldness and that of his commanders on that day would be matched only by the success they would achieve on the following day.

At 0400 on 16 May 40, Pz.A.A.37, under Major Erdmann, occupied Froidchapelle in preparation for the attack later in the day through the French frontier fortifications and deep behind the Allied forces in Belgium. At 1430, in accordance with the order of Hoth as commanding general of XV.A.K. (mot.), Rommel moved the division toward the French fortified zone and the city of Avesnes, approximately 35 km from Froidchapelle on the other side of the frontier defenses. Preceded by Pz.AA.37, the division occupied the Belgian town of Sivry close to the border and concentrated A.R.78 (*Artillerie Regiment* 78) and a battery of 37mm Flak to support the attack. Rommel positioned Pz.R.25 in Sivry close to the head of the division and then sent Pz.A.A37 over the French border. At 1800, Pz.R.25, accompanied by Rommel moved out in the attack on the French fortified zone. At Clairfoyts, 2 km into France, the Panzer regiment ran into the French fortifications. The battle was on.

---

22. Ibid., Fr. 000689.

After approximately 5 hours of combat led by pioneers, K.7 and Pz.A.A.37, the division had worked its way through the last road obstacles west of Clairfoyts. At 2300 almost in the middle of the night, Rommel personally led a powerful *Vorausabteilung* (advanced detachment) of the division consisting of K.7 (minus one company), Pz.A.A.37, and Pz.R.25, into France west of Clairfoyts. Increasing the tempo once again, motorcycles, armored reconnaissance cars, and tanks advanced at 2300. Division artillery screened their flanks and carpeted the roads and villages in front of the advanced detachment with fire. As Rommel and the strong advanced detachment reached within approximately 10 km of the day's target, the city of Avesnes, it came under flanking fire from French artillery in positions on both sides of the route of advance. According to the German combat record of the confrontation, this dangerous barrage was silenced by "broadsides out of the barrels of all of the weapons" while the column continued to drive along the road.[23] This bold action was vintage Rommel. It was probably based on his experience of World War I from which he had extracted the rule that in a meeting engagement the side wins that fires first the most rounds in the direction of the enemy.[24]

Minutes later, at about 2300, Pz.R.25 thrust into the rear of a column of a French mechanized division with large numbers of enemy motorized troops and tanks in parking areas alongside the road. Maintaining the same tempo, and continuing to fire from the road, the tanks of Pz.R.25 moved through the middle of French troops no longer able to offer effective resistance to the Germans with their surprise presence deep in a supposedly secure rear area. At midnight and now 75 km west of the Meuse, the tanks of Pz.R.25 with Rommel among them drove through the streets of Avesnes and seized the heights to

---

23. *7.Pz.D., Ia, Kurzberichte: Der Kampf im Westen, Mai-Juni 1940*, U.S. Archives, German Records, Divisions, T-315, Roll 401, Fr. 000691.

24. See in General Field Marshal Erwin Rommel, *Infantry Attacks* (Quantico, VA, 1956), p. 109. This work is a reprint of a 1943 translation of *Infanterie Greift* an originally published in Potsdam in 1937.

the west of it. The French around Avesnes collapsed. Under Major Crasemann, II./A.R.78, for example, which had managed to stay close behind Pz.R.25 captured 48 French tanks intact. Many French troops fled weaponless to the north and south spreading panic and uncertainty among other troops. German casualties, which had been heavy in the tough fighting at the Meuse (e.g., from 12-15 May 40 totalling 150 KIA, 481 WIA, and 6 MIA), fell to four killed and 16 wounded for 16 May 40.[25] The Germans would capture approximately 6,000 French troops in the following morning hours of 17 May.[26] (See Figures 12 and 13 for a running account of German and French losses on pages 30 and 31).

On 16 May 40, 7.Pz.D. had contact with its neighboring units to the north and south only through radio transmissions, and 32.1.D. now approximately 45 km behind 7.Pz.D. could no longer really be considered a "neighboring unit." Since the onset of darkness on the evening of 16 May 40, to compound matters, there had been no radio contact between the division commander up front with the tanks of Pz.R.25, or the operations staff of the division or the artillery or Schtz. Brig.7 (Schutzen Brigade 7, a headquarters element controlling S.R.7 and S.R.6). The situation developed into an impressive illustration of the chance and uncertainty of war - essentially chaos - and the way in which a leader of genius using a military system of superior merit brought success out of chaos.

No longer in contact with Rommel, and not imagining he had already seized Avesnes, Schtz.Brig.7 moved its headquarters and S.R.6 into rest positions near Sivry, approximately 20 km back from Rommel's actual location in and around Avesnes. The brigade also directed S.R.7 into *rest* positions where it was located even farther

---

25. Ibid., *Gefangenen und Beute*, Fn. 000857.
26. See the summary in, *7.Pz.D., Ia, Geschichte der 7.Pz.Div., Kurzer Abriss uber den Einsatz im Westen, 9. Mai-19. Juni, 1940, Verluste der 7. Panzer-Division*, U.S. Archives, German Records, Division, T-315, Roll 401, Fr. 000859.

DATE	KIA			WIA			MIA		
	0	NCO	E	0	NCO	E	0	NCO	E
10 May	-	1	1	1	-	7	-	-	-
11 May	-	-	3	-	1	6	-	1	2
12 May	3	6	15	5	8	33	-	-	-
13 May	4	7	49	15	40	167	-	1	5
14 May	3	7	41	10	33	114	-	-	-
15 May	-	-	15	1	12	43	-	-	-
16 May	-	-	4	1	5	10	-	-	-
17 May	2	6	28	3	18	38	-	-	-
18 May	4	9	22	6	13	51	-	-	7
19 May	0	5	10	1	1	26	-	2	7
20 May	1	5	45	1	20	116	-	-	5
21 May	7	17	65	4	26	86	1	24	148
22 May	3	1	14	1	3	32	1	1	45
23 May	-	1	19	-	3	17	-	-	-
24 May	1	1	9	1	5	52	1	2	3
25 May	-	-	1	-	-	-	-	-	-
26 May	1	3	9	2	11	30	-	-	2
27 May	1	4	30	3	19	72	-	-	-
28 May	2	-	7	1	4	12	-	-	-
29 May	-	-	2	1	-	13	-	-	3
30 May	-	-	3	-	-	3	-	-	-
31 May	-	-	-	-	3	-	-	-	-
1 June	-	1	-	-	-	1	-	-	-
2-4 June	-	-	-	-	-	-	-	-	-
5 June	3	10	55	6	29	119	-	-	-
6 June	3	8	10	4	11	41	-	-	-
7 June	-	-	4	-	3	11	-	-	-
8-9 June	3	4	11	1	10	16	-	-	-
10 June	-	-	3	2	8	25	-	-	-
11 June	2	3	15	1	5	28	-	-	-
12 June	2	5	20	1	9	27	-	-	-
13 June	-	1	-	-	3	-	-	-	-
14 June	-	-	-	-	-	-	-	-	-
15 June	-	-	-	-	-	-	-	-	-
16 June	0	1	6	3	1	8	-	-	-
17-19 June	3	2	18	2	12	47	-	-	-
20-21 June	-	-	1	-	1	1	-	-	-
22 June	-	-	1	-	-	-	-	-	-
	48	108	536	77	317	1252	3	34	227

Figure 12. Casualties of 7.Pz.D. in Battle of France, (10 May - 22 June 1940).

DATE	PRISONERS	GUNS (Incl. AA)	TANKS	AT GUNS	AIRCRAFT
10 May	30	-	-	-	1
11 May	13	-	-	-	2
12 May	10	-	4	3	2
13 May	345	-	4	-	6
14 May	160	8	7	4	-
15 May	450	18	75	-	3
16 May	-	-	-	-	-
17 May	10,000	27	100	-	2
18 May	100	-	5	-	22
19 May	650	-	-	-	1
20 May	500	-	5	5	6
21 May	50	-	43	-	1
22 May	50	-	16	-	4
23 May	50	-	11	-	-
24 May	50	-	10	-	-
25 May	20	-	-	-	-
26 May	190	-	2	-	-
27 May	600	12	15	-	-
28 May	950	23	10	-	-
29 May	150	-	-	-	-
5 June	1,000	52	5	30	-
6 June	1,500	-	24	-	6
7 June	1,500	16	-	-	4
8-9 June	1,400	12	10	-	15
10 June	500	13	24	-	-
11 June	1,200	-	-	-	-
12 June	46,000	73	58	22	4
17-19 June	30,000	23	-	-	-
	97,468	277	428	64	79

Figure 13. Allied Losses in Combat with 7.Pz.D., (10 May - 19 June 1940).

to the rear. Hoth, XV.A.K. (mot.), also out of contact with Rommel, ordered 7.Pz.D. to resume the attack against Avesnes. As this chaotic situation developed - chaotic in the sense of being based on false (and irrelevant) premises - Rommel remained in touch with operational reality and the opportunity and danger of the situation. He was able to ignore the operational dangers and seize the operational opportunity because of his location with the leading elements of a division on the offensive. During the course of the night, he had no "exchange of ideas" with the Ia and had only the most general impression of where the mass of the division was located; nevertheless, he resolved with characteristic initiative to continue the attack to the west with the entire division *before the break of day*. He intended to seize the bridge over the Sambre River at Landrecies 18 km farther to the west and hold it open for the rest of the German army.

In the meantime, the French revived in Avesnes. Pz.R.25 with K7 and Pz A.A.37 faced several hours of street fighting and mechanized attack in the immediate countryside in which the German 37mm *Pak* and tank guns had little effect against the strong armor of the French tanks. The Germans finally mastered this crisis with the intervention of *Panzer IV* tanks of Pz.R.25 from the rear firing the stronger armor piercing ammunition from the short 75mm cannon on those tanks. Rommel, Rothenburg and the strong advanced detachment of the division attacked at 0530 17 May 40 toward Landrecies and immediately ran into columns of French motor vehicles both on and alongside of the road used for the advance. Astonished by the presence of the German tanks and motorcyclists, the French soldiers gave up in large numbers and slowed the German advance by their "administrative" presence and crowding along the road. The advanced detachment, nonetheless, reached Landrecies at approximately 0600 and took the bridge over the Sambre River undamaged.

Oberst Rothenburg thrust beyond the Sambre to the communications center at Le Cateau 10 km farther west where the advance came to a halt on the eastern outskirts of that city. At this juncture, Rommel was forced to acknowledge that between Landrecies and Le Cateau he had only two tiring tank battalions of Pz.R.25 and part of K.7. The rest of the advanced detachment - Pz.A.A.37 and the remainder of K.7 and the tanks - were in the area from Landrecies back towards Avesnes, and the mass of the division still somewhere *east* of Landrecies, i.e., approximately 30-50 km distant from Rothenburg and his tanks in the foremost positions. In this uncomfortable situation requiring a shift to the defensive to consolidate the finger projecting deeply behind the Allied armies in Belgium, Rommel drove back from the advanced positions in an armored reconnaissance vehicle 28 km to Avesnes. Now in radio and physical contact with the mass of the division, he pushed forward S.R.6, S.R.7, and the division artillery of A.R.78 to defend the area of the projecting linger.

On the afternoon of 17 May 40, Hoth compounded Rommel's difficult situation through a directive that showed brilliant flexibility on the part of that operationally agile and bold commander. As corps commander, Hoth ordered 7.Pz.D. to take the bridge over the Sambre at Berlaimont 13 km *northwest* of Avesnes in a direction eccentric to the main attack of the division westward through Le Cateau. Hoth gave the division the mission to seize the bridge there and hold it open so that 5.Pz.D., Rommel's neighbor to the north and still about a day behind 7.Pz.D. would have the opportunity to catch up and advance parallel with and adjacent to Rommel. The operations staff, 7.Pz.D., sent off I./S.R.6 under *Oberleutnant* Kiessling reinforced by II./A.R.78, a modest sized task force that would successfully accomplish its mission and incidentally contribute to Kiessling winning the E.K. I that day. Advanced elements of 5.Pz.D. moved into the bridgehead during the evening of 17 May 40. *Generalmajor* Lemelsen, the commander of 5.Pz.D., would appear to have closed the distance between the two Panzer divisions by getting advanced elements across the Sambre by that time. In actuality, by the same time, Rommel had concentrated the mass of 7.Pz.D. close to the Sambre and still lay effectively about 30 km west of his neighbor.

Rommel and 7.Pz.D. advanced with a style that is brought out in some of the message traffic of 17 May 40. Similarly to his request for air attack out in front of the division along its route of advance in the run through Philippeville two days earlier, Rommel would request through XV.A.K. (mot.) Stukas out in front of his advance (See Figures 14, 15, in appendix). Rommel seems to have seen special, useful effects through disorganization and scattering of French units along the route of advance and especially the suppression of the highly regarded French artillery. During darkness at 0325, Rommel sent a message that nicely illustrates the style of a successful commander of a mobile division in the attack. Rommel sent the succinct, decisive message somewhat ominously as being from the "General" and to the Division Command Post. In it, the sender states simply: "Rommel up front in a tank." (See Figure 16, in appendix.) At the time Rommel was forward personally seeing to the details of getting the attack going on schedule at 0430 and transferring a sense of urgency to all those around him. The commanding general of 7.Pz.Div. held the initiative against a tough but badly shaken enemy. He was forward in a tank with the most advanced element of the division: no man around him could doubt that great events were about to unfold.

The situation had its advantages and disadvantages. Rommel stood completely free of the command post bureaucracy modest though it was in 7.Pz.D. and its distance from the shooting, but he was also out of contact with his own operations staff and the rest of the division, his neighbors, and corps headquarters. Combat against the enemy, as opposed to contact with staffs and headquarters, would take place with the tanks of Pz.R.25. Rommel advanced with those tanks and forced combat on the French at a time and place of his choosing. Physically located in the middle of the decisive combat taking place in the sector of 7.Pz.D., Rommel could make decisions fast - decisions that also would be in touch with the realities of combat at the crucial point in the battle. The road to defeat is probably paved more thickly with missed opportunity than any other factor; Rommel and 7.Pz.D. let few combat opportunities slip away from them because: "Rommel up front in a tank."

Hoth at the command post of XV.A.K. (mot.) ordered 7.Pz.D. to attack through Le Cateau toward Cambrai at 0900 18 May 40. The French, however, fought back vigorously around Pommereuil (between Landrecies and Le Cateau) and Headquarters XV.A.K. (mot.) ordered 7.Pz.D. to shift its axis of advance south to allow 5.Pz.D. to begin to move from Landrecies through Le Cateau. Hard working and successful, 7.Pz.D. had been directed earlier to seize bridgeheads over the Sambre at Landrecies and Berlaimont on 16 May 40. Corps headquarters now, in effect, directed 7.Pz.D. to turn over those crossing to the slower 5.Pz.D. and shift its axis of advance to new sites south of Landrecies. Without a chance of meeting the 0900 time for an attack around Le Cateau, Rommel ordered S.R.7 and Pz.A.A.37 each (i.e., two axes for the new attack over the Sambre) at a different location to make a crossing of the river. These attacks met strong resistance and required pioneer support. In the meantime, S.R.6 around Pommereuil encountered strong resistance also in its attempt to finish off scattered French forces still capable of organized resistance in the midst of the division there.

Rommel began the main advance west not until around 1700 18 May 40 and organized it around two battle groups. He directed Pz.R.25, K.7 and I./S.r. 6 reinforced with artillery and Flak to attack north of *Route Nationale 39* with the objective to seize the communications center of Cambrai. S.R. 7 was directed to advance out of its new bridgehead farther south and attack towards Cambrai parallel with *Route Nationale 39* and just south of it. Although Pz.R.25 had been momentarily weakened by fuel and tank ammunition shortages, the attack immediately made good progress. While Pz.R.25 thrust into the outskirts of Cambrai by the onset of darkness (approximately 2100), Rommel ordered K.7 and I./S.R. 6 under *Major* von Paris and reinforced by a few tanks and a Flak platoon to skirt Cambrai to the north and seize the bridges over the L'Escant Canal there. The attack succeeded. Pz.R.25 met difficulties, however, with strong obstacles in the outskirts of Cambrai and pulled out of the city directly to the east.

In the meantime during the night, S.R. 7 took the area immediately to the southeast and south of Cambrai. 7.Pz.D. had bowled over the French again in a late afternoon and early evening advance.

The situation remained fluid, tense, and uncertain, nevertheless, as the Germans faced strong French counterattacks with tanks 24 km back from Cambrai around Le Cateau. With tough persistence, the French mounted tank and infantry attacks from the north against Landrecies, the original bridgehead across the Sambre. The latter attacks threatened the whole German position west of the river forcing the Division Ia (*Major i.G.* Heidkamper) to commit an entire pioneer battalion (Pi.Btl.624 from corps troops) to the defense in support of II./S.R. 6 and most of the division artillery. Shifting to the defensive everywhere by around midnight, the division also faced a difficult night in getting through fuel and ammunition to the forward elements at Cambrai. Map 2, in appendix, illustrates the situation on the evening of 18 May 40 as sketched in on a 1:25,000 scale map by the Ia of the division.[27]

The sketch shows the extraordinary situation created by the success of 7.Pz.D.. The adjacent division to the south - now 12.1.D. - lay 52 km behind the motorcyclists and motorized infantry of 7.Pz.D. now west of the L'Escant Canal. The 5.Pz.D. still lay along the Sambre in a large bridgehead 29 km behind the units of its neighbor across the canal. The powerful German armored forces in *Panzer-Gruppe* Kleist would soon move in alongside of Rommel's division to the south of it. Kleist's forces in XIXA.K. (mot.) shown on the map as 2.Pz.D., I.Pz.D., and 29. (mot.) lay roughly as far west as Rommel's division but would be outstripped again by the advance of 7.Pz.D. on 20 May 40. The German army, in effect, advanced along two main axes in terms of actual success achieved - the intended main axis of *Panzer-Gruppe*

---

27. *7.Pz.D., Ia, Geschichte der 7.Pz.Div., Kurzer Abriss uber den Einsatz im Westen, 9 Mai-19 Juni, 1940, Lage an 18.5 abends*, U.S. Archives, German Records, Divisions, T-315, Roll 401, Fr. 000788.

Kleist and specifically XIX.A.K. (mot.) (*General der Panzertruppe H. Guderian*) and the unintended but equally successful advance of 7.Pz.D.. As Map 2 suggests, the German penetrations served to break up the French front.

During the long daylight hours of 19 May 40, 7.Pz.D. prepared for a continuation of the attack westward to Arras and then north- west to the English Channel. Rommel ordered S.R. 7 which had seized the area south of Cambrai to establish another bridgehead across the L'Escant Canal in order for the division to continue its attack along two axes. The regiment succeeded in the afternoon in crossing the canal and establishing a bridgehead just to the south-west of Cambrai. By 1800 19 May 40, 8.Pz.D. had moved up alongside of 7.Pz.D. with its right flank now about 5 km south of Cambrai. Farther to the rear, Pz.AA.37 which had been screening 7.Pz.D. to the south of Le Cateau was relieved by a *Waffen S.S.* regiment, one of several formed in time to fight in France and a high quality, fully motorized unit. Pz.A.A.34 moved west to Cambrai to join in the post-midnight attack of the division toward Arras.

At 0140 20 May 40, 7.Pz.D. moved out of its bridgeheads north and south of Cambrai in an advance along French national route 39 to Arras. Rommel organized the attacking division into two columns with Pz.R.25 as the mass of the northern column. Using the term, "escort" to describe his presence with Rothenburg at Pz.R.25, Rommel moved out personally with the tanks in the attack. The great obstacle to be negotiated in order to get to Arras was the *Canal du Nord* 10 km west of Cambrai at Marquion. The German tanks reached the canal before daybreak at 0300 but an alert Anglo-French security force blew up the bridge in the face of Pz.R.25. Two hours later several kilometers south of Marquion, the German tank units managed to seize an intact bridge and push across the canal. The tanks were accompanied by the S.J.G. Kompanie (heavy Infantry Gun Company, or s.J.G.Kp.) of Hauptmann Fischer, a special unit of 105mm "infantry guns" or in artillery parlance, howitzers. The guns were mounted in armored boxes on the tracked chassis of the Panzer I 5-ton training tank of the 1930s. About two hours later, Pz.R.25 and the self propelled heavy infantry guns reached Beaurains, 3 km directly south af Arras. Rommel, who had personally escorted the advance, ordered the tank regiment to stop there when it became evident that the mass of the division had not followed the tanks.

Protected by a tank and an armored reconnaissance car, Rommel, the division commander himself, set out to the rear to find out the reason for the broken connection and bring forward the mass of the division. Approximately halfway back to the *Canal du Nord*, Rommel and his security element encountered French heavy tanks which knocked out both of the German armored vehicles. Rommel and his remaining radio and security personnel survived by lying low while surrounded by French tanks and infantry for several hours. Later in the morning, the rest of 7.Pz.D. would advance through the town of Vis en Artois where Rommel's detachment had been hit, and Rommel would be saved. Map 3 in appendix illustrates the situation of the division in the campaign at approximately 0700 20 May 40 or the time that Rommel was attacked.[28] The map shows a long fingerlike projection that illustrates the special qualities of Rommel in keeping forces on the offensive moving. It also shows a long northern flank exposed to strong Anglo-French forces retreating toward the Belgian coast but tempted to breakthrough southward into France.

For the remainder of the day, 7.Pz.D. fought off counter-attacks from the north and organized a defense of the exposed northern flank. The operations staff requested a *Waffen S.S.* battalion from the *S.S. Division Totenkopf* (Death's Head Division) newly constituted and in process of being inserted in combat on the western front bewtwen 7.

---

28.   *7.Pz.D., Ia, Geschichte der 7.Pz.Div., Kurzer Abriss uber den Einsatz im Westen, 9 Mai-19 Juni, 1940, Lage c. 0700 20.5.40*, U.S., Archives, German Records, Divisions, T-315, Roll 4-1, Fr. 000794.

and 8.pz.D.. The operations staff would use the *Waffen S.S.* battalion to fill in the "lengthening" northern flank of 7.Pz.D.. During the remainder of 20 May 40, K.7 and Pz.AA37 would endure severe counterattacks from the north, Pi.B.58 would construct a 16-ton capacity bridge over the *Canal du Nord*, and Rommel would begin to organize a great final dash around Arras and on to the coast now only about 87 km away. The day had been another one of tough fighting - the division had lost another 51 men killed, 137 wounded, and 5 missing in action. Heavy casualties such as these support a view that the French Campaign involved severe combat and contradict the view that the Germans had a quick, easy campaign. The campaign was quick but costly and challenging with severe fighting.

Rommel exchanged messages with various elements of the division on 20 May 40; these messages help bring the German style of advance into focus. The attack from Cambrai to Arras began in total darkness at 0140 and shortly afterward at 0202 Rommel was positioned 8.5 km east of the bridge across the *Canal du Nord* west of the outskirts of Cambrai. Rommel and the tanks of Pz.R.25 under Rothenburg advanced through darkness and French resistance to reach Marquion and the disaster of a destroyed bridge over the canal. Rommel's brief message to the division command post says it all. In a message of almost the same time Rommel queries the command post on the location of S.R.6 and S.R.7 which were supposed to be advancing alongside of Pz.R.25 in the southern column of the attacking force. By 0355, facing the disaster of being completely stopped by the water barrier, and wasting few words, Rommel ordered Rothenburg and Pz.R.25 into position to the south of the bridge to attempt to force a crossing and *Major* von Paris, I./S.R.6 accompanying the tank-heavy column, to move into positions to the north. Note the ultra brief, urgent style of command (See Figures 17, 18, 19, in appendix):

MESSAGE			
Date	Time	From-To	Message Wording
20.5	0202	General to Div Staff	Rommel 34 2 einhalb km rechts, (Rommel located 34 2 1/2 km right)[29]
20.5	0300	General to Div Staff	Rommel Wo 6 and 7 (Rommel Where are S.R.6 and S.R.7?).[30]
20.5	0305	General to Div Staff	Rommel 44 1/2 Brucke gesprengt 100 Gefangen Keine Gegenwehr (Rommel 44 1/2 bridge blown up 100 prisoners no resistance).[31]

In the first message, Rommel personally told the division staff that he was located forward in the field at 34 km along the thrust line of the day and 2.5 km to the right of it. Rommel was moving with his own radio vehicle and also using Pz.R.25 radios as appropriate. In the second message, Rommel asked for the location of S.R.6 and S.R.7. The time of the message (0300) is important; he had just encountered the destroyed bridge over the canal and wanted to know immediately the location of the motorized infantry regiments in order to exploit any possibilities in their advance farther south. In the last message, in the absence of a written record of the location of the thrust line for the day, he told future analysts exactly where point 44 1/2 lay on the thrust line toward Arras, namely, at the bridge over the *Canal du Nord* at Marquion. Rommel also told us that no resistance was being encountered, doubling the irony of a successfully blown bridge, i.e., the enemy had successfully destroyed the bridge but had prepared no resistance on the French side. Rommel had to move fast to exploit this fleeting opportunity. One senses this in the following messages (Figures 20, 21, 22, 23, in appendix):

---

29. *7.Pz.D., Ia, Anlagen zum Krlegstagebuch: Operationsakten. 20.5.40, Nr. 109,* U.S. Archives, German Records, Divisions, T-315, Role 403, Fr. 000006.

30. Ibid., *Nr. 112,* Fr. 000013.

31. Ibid., *Nr. 112,* Fr. 000022.

MESSAGE			
Date	Time	From-To	Message Wording
20.5	0400	General to Div Staff	Rommel Pioniere nach vorne (Rommel directs: Pioneers to the front).[32]
20.5	0415	General to Div Staff	Rommel Teile der Artillerie in Stellung bringen in Linie 43 1 km rechts bis 43 2 km links. (Rommel directs: bring part of the artillery into position 43 right 1 to 43 left 2).[33]

MESSAGE			
Date	Time	From-To	Message Wording
20.5	0445	Artillery Commander to The General	Craseman geht 43 links in Stellung, welchen Auftrag? (Major Crasemann has gone into position 43 left, what is the mission?).[34]
20.5	0530	General to Div Staff	Rommel Bruckenbau 44 1/2 dringend notig. Pion. beschleunigt durchfuhren. Rommel jetzt 46 1 km links geht vorwarts (Rommel sends: bridge construction urgently necessary. Pioneers expedite moving up. Rommel presently at 46 1 km left goes forward).[35]

To get to Arras on 20 May 40, Rommel and 7.Pz.D. had to use their developing style of the daily, quick, indeed almost "instantaneous" bound forward. At 0300, Rommel was in serious trouble for the day facing a navigable canal, i.e., a deep water obstacle with specially constructed obstacle-like banks and, of course, no fords, with the bridge to his front destroyed. Rommel and the division depended for their success on a special tempo of operational movement; immobility

32. *7.Pz.D., Ia, Anlagen zum Kriegstagebuch: Operationsakten. 20.5.40, Nr. 117*, U.S. Archives, German Records, Division, T-315, Roll 403, Fr. 000025.

33. Ibid., *Nr. 118*, Fr. 000028.

34. Ibid., *Nr. 121*, Fr. 000032.

35. Ibid., *Nr. 121*, Fr. 000035.

and a well advertised presence made the division a magnet for enemy reserves and accompanying counterattacks. Rommel immediately ordered the two heavy maneuver elements of his column, to deploy around the destroyed bridge, Pz.R.25 to the south and I./S.R.6 to the north, and find a crossing. As Rommel discovered that S.R.6 and 7 were not alongside to the south, the search widened to the south for a crossing. He also realized the fundamental necessity to get bridges built and repaired at Marquion as soon as possible. With inimitable brevity Rommel directed "pioneers to the front."

As the division momentarily began to face the problem of a possible opposed river crossing, Rommel began to prepare for the worst. As a commander of a mobile force in a hurry and surrounded by chaos both potential and immediate, Rommel directed the division staff (essentially the Ia and the "artillery commander") with inspiring regard for their competence, to bring into position "part of the artillery" anywhere it chose in a general area designated by him. Everyone seems to speak the same language. With equally inspiring regard for the urgency of the situation transferred by the division commander, the artillery commander moves first and then, as laconically as Rommel, queries:

7.Pz.D. Message		
Date	**Time**	**Rommel's Location (on Division Thrust Line)**
20.5	0113	34 Rommel near Cambrai
20.5	0550	34 Rommel near Cambrai
20.5	0606	c.44 Rommel at Marquion
20.5	0620	44 Rommel still at Marquion
20.5	0650	46 Rommel just south N39 enroute Arras
20.5	0754	50 Rommel just south N39 enroute Arras
20.5	0202	57 Rommel west of Vis en Artois
20.5	0305	71 Rommel west of Vis en Artois
20.5	0501	58 Rommel west of Vis en Artois

"What's the mission?" About 15 minutes after this exchange, Pz.R.25 discovered and began to move across a passable bridge several kilometers to the south of Marquion. Shortly after the beginning of the passage of the canal at about 0500, Rommel sent a wordy message by his standards reiterating the "urgent necessity" for pioneers and a passable big bridge at Marquion on the direct route to Arras.

At this point a remarkable advance began which sheds light on the German style in offensive operations. On 20 May 40, 7.Pz.D., from 0100-2400 on that day, would advance from Cambrai to the area just west of Arras. The Germans moved during that readily gauged period - one day - an impressive 40 km. The Germans played an operational trick during this day because most of it they spent organizing defenses to the north, fighting off counter-attacks, and generally tidying up in the area of their surge forward.

The times show Rommel leading an advance from Cambrai to Marquion on the *Canal du Nord* 10 km forward in a scant, approximate 1.5 hours. The Germans were then delayed for about 2 hours looking for a passable crossing of the canal. Once Rothenburg in Pz.R.25 found that crossing, he, Rommel, and the tanks and self propelled infantry guns accelerated an astounding 27 km (i.e., from 34 on the division thrust line to 71) to Beaurains by 0650 or approximately 1 hour and 50 minutes after crossing the canal. The analysis shows that during the 24-hour or "one-day" period in which 7.Pz.D. gets historical credit for advancing from Cambrai to Arras, the advance took place largely from 0500 to 0650.

The following day, 21 May 40, Headquarters XXXIX.A.K. (mot.), now in control of 7.Pz.D., ordered the division to attack around Arras to the west of it and then head directly north toward the English Channel. *Generalleutnant* Schmidt ordered the attack for 1030 and the division moved out promptly, with Pz.R.25 leading, followed by Pz.R.6 in column to the right and Pz.R.7 in column to the left. As had been the case since the first day of the campaign, 7.Pz.D. almost immediately formed a deep penetration into enemy country with no German neighbors to the east (Arras) or west. Directly to the rear of the division lay 5.Pz.D. in no position to advance behind 7.Pz.D. and provide support. To the left of 7.Pz.D., loosely connected, somewhat behind, and concerned about its own front lay the mildly nervous, untried, but tough and aggressive new *Waffen S.S. Division Totenkopf.* By 1530 21 May 40, 7.Pz.D had formed another deep fingerlike projection now heading north northwest and approximately 10 km long.

At that moment, strong British and French forces attacked 7.Pz.D.'s lengthy flank. The attack came across an impressively wide front of approximately 8 km. The Allied force attacked with about 144 tanks (74 British, 70 French) including a number of heavily armored British tanks that were impervious to the German standard 37mm *Pak* of the day. The Allied attack hit against the extremely extended units of S.R.6. Five batteries of 105mm light field howitzers from A.R.78. 1./S.R.6, under Major von Paris, took the most casualties of any German battalion-level organization and was partly overrun. The Allied forces that pushed through I./S.R.6 ran into German artillery, *Pak* of Pz.Jg.42, units of S.R.7 and troops of the neighboring *Waffen S.S. Division Totenkopf.* The Allied forces did not run into any German tanks because virtually all of them were several kilometers to the north and well in advance of the motorized infantry. Between 1530 and 1900 21 May, 7.Pz.D. used direct artillery, Flak, and *Pak* fire to halt the Allied attack. Division artillery, alone for example, succeeded in putting out of action 25 Allied tanks. As the attack developed, Rommel found himself in the middle of it and personally organized the fire of numerous weapons including light Flak around him. Rommel also ordered *Oberst* Rothenburg to turn about Pz.R.25 and attack the Allies on their northern flank. Rothenburg began his drive back down from north of the battle area about 2000, ran into a strong British defensive front and lost nine battle tanks (3 *Panzer IV* and 6 *Panzer 38(f)*), but Rothenburg broke through and reached the area where the heaviest part of the Allied attack had originated.

Rothenburg reached this area about 2300 21 May 40 and through this counterattack stabilized the German defenses.

7.Pz.D. suffered heavy casualties in the fighting totalling 89 KIA, 116 WIA, and 173 MIA. The figure for missing probably includes mostly personnel captured with a significant percentage of those taken prisoner being wounded. The division lost nine battle tanks and approximately four additional light tanks. Characteristically for the Germans, they claimed Allied losses with restraint and candor, for example 43 Allied tanks "destroyed," probably an accurate figure based on the Germans reoccupying the area in which the combat had taken place. Such was the balance of combat power in the campaign that 7.Pz.D. would go on the next morning to continue the drive north toward the English Channel and suffer both the success and frustration of the fighting around Dunkirk toward the end of May.

7.Pz.D. would continue on in the French Campaign to great success in its attack across the Somme near the channel coast on 5 June 40, the prevention of a little Dunkirk-style evacuation of Allied troops around St. Valery, and the dash from the Seine River to Cherbourg in the last days of the battle. By that time, however, the Germans had been so successful in their offensive particularly from 10-21 May 40, that it is difficult to grant the Allies much chance of survival in the campaign. The fairest time and most instructive to gauge the German advance is probably during the time when the Allies were strongest in the campaign and the Germans still had appreciable chances of losing. The advance of 7.Pz.D. from about 12-21 May 40 should give analysts today insights into effective style and technique in war fighting.

The entire campaign, of course, remains important and it is significant to note that the high command of the German Army (*Oberkommando des Heeres*, or OKH) distributed a questionnaire at the end of the campaign to the Army Groups on the battle in the west. Army Group B, under which 7.Pz.D. was included at the end of the campaign, passed on the questionnaire to its subordinate units on 7 July 40 only a short time after the end of the fighting. 7.Pz.D. answered the various questions in a report of 19 July 40 that contains some interesting insights into the style of a German mobile formation. The German advance in the west can be likened in many ways to a long series of river crossings. Not surprisingly, the Ia, 7.Pz.Div. in presenting the experiences of the division dwelt on river crossing operations and presented the view that a mobile division must have *two* complete bridging columns in its pioneer company. The Ia pointed out that a mobile division would often be faced with crossing a second major water barrier before it could retrieve its bridging column set in place on the previous barrier. The Ia also presented the view that the motorized infantry regiments and motorcycle battalion should be equipped with light and heavy pneumatic rubber boats for flexibility in immediate negotiation of water barriers by assault infantry and various light weapons and vehicles on rafts put together from those boats.

In comments on maintaining communications amongst the various parts of the division, the Ia noted that the division commander positioned himself with the leading formation, most often the tank regiment, and found himself in the thick of combat. The Ia made the point that the combat operations staff and radio communications personnel of the division commander must be "under armor" in such circumstances. This comment suggests that for a Marine division in a mobile offensive operation, the division commander must think in terms of a small combat staff around him with adequate communications in vehicles that have the "battlefield mobility" to move and survive with the most mobile ground elements of the division.

As the spearhead of the army in which it was organized, 7.Pz.D. came under extensive air attack throughout the campaign. The organic and attached Flak units of the division, for example, are credited with shooting down 31 Allied aircraft in the brief period examined in this study from 10-21 May 40. Assuming that these aircraft were engaged in attacks against the division and that larger numbers of attacking aircraft were not shot down, one can state that 7.Pz.D. came under *heavy* air attack during its advance by no fewer than 31 Allied aircraft and probably a *much larger* figure. Faced with this experience - heavy air attack but an impressive number of them shot down - the Ia noted that the division had adequate Flak in its war organization but that there was a pressing necessity for some kind of fighter detachment to be on station over the division.

General der Infanterie (General of the Infantry, equivalent to U.S. Lieutenant General) Hermann Hoth, who commanded the German XV.A.K. (mot.), wrote a brief paper of 17 November 40 summarizing the exploits of his corps in the French Campaign largely in terms of the performance of 7.Pz.D.. He notes though that the extraordinary achievements of 7.Pz.D. was only part of a larger whole: "the deed of the individual is silent; success and failure of a particular troop unit is not decisive; above all, the significance of a success of arms reveals itself with relationship to the overall operation of the army. Indeed of the whole armed forces."[36] The statement reveals a lot about Hoth as a commander of a German armored corps (in 1940 still designated Army Corps (motorized) or A.K.(mot.)) and about the style and thinking processes of the German army. In it, Hoth warns the reader that the exploits of his corps, 7.Pz.D., and Rommel, are important predominately in terms of their contribution to overall victory in the Battle of France. In it, also, the German army reveals itself as one which placed a premium on officers like Hoth and Rommel, who visualized their actions in terms of the next higher command.

The German army shows itself, then as one dedicated to effects that contributed to the general mission. In that army, for example, combat

---

36. *7.Pz.Div., Ia, Gefechts-und Erfahrungsberichte, 31.5.-29.11. 1940, Der Kommandierende General XVA.K., K. Gef. St., den* 17.11.40, p. 1, U.S., National Archives, Records of German Field Commands, Divisions, Microcopy T-315, Roll 436, Frame 000619 (hereinafter, U.S., Ar-chives, German Records, Divisions, T-315, Roll, Fr.).

soldiers won decorations according to a mission oriented logic: the army awarded decorations according to actions affecting the overall situation. German private soldiers did not get the *Ritterkreuz* (Knight's Cross, or rough equivalent of the U.S. Congressional Medal of Honor) for falling on hand grenades. Except on exceedingly rare occasion in the entire Second World War, German private soldiers were not awarded the Knight's Cross.[37] The German army awarded it almost exclusively to officers, not for reasons of feudal sociology, but based on the ruthless and consistent logic that the higher decoration must reflect action affecting the accomplishment of the general mission. The Germany army would award the Knight's Cross to Rommel for leading 7.Pz.D. in the Battle of France. Its next lower decoration - the *Eiserne Kreuz I* (*E.K.* I or Iron Cross First Class) - was reserved largely for officers and a handful of private soldiers in World War II. For the first great day of battle in the French Campaign, 13 May 40, comprising the crossing of the Meuse River, 7.Pz.D. would award 16 E.K. I distributed as follows by rank:

13 May 40, Crossing the Meuse, E.K. I Awards[38]

Officers	7
Staff Sergeants	6
Sergeants	3
(Privates & Corporals)	0
Total	**16**

Operating in an army that emphasized the general picture in battle, Hoth goes on self-effacingly to state that the *Hauptstoss*, or major effort, of the entire German armed forces in the western offensive

---

37.   In the *Waffen S.S.* which fought alongside of the army, numbering nearly 750,000 men at the end of World War II, and reflecting a decoration mentality more "democratic" than the army, the command authority awarded only a small percentage to private soldiers, i.e., U.S. equivalent of privates and corporals.

38.   See in, *7.Pz.D., Ia, Kurzberichte: Der Kampf im Westen, Mai-June 1940*, U.S. Archives, German Records, Divisions, T-315, Roll 401, Fr. 000684.

lay with the mobile divisions (i.e., the panzer and motorized infantry divisions) massed south of him under command of *General der Kavallerie* Ewald von Kleist in *Panzer-Gruppe von Kleist* (Panzer Group Kleist). Hoth makes it clear that his corps had the mission to protect the right flank of Panzer Group Kleist against an attack by powerful Allied forces that would be located farther north in Belgium. He notes specifically that such an attack "would bring into question the reaching of the channel coast,"[39] thus preventing the accomplishment of the overall mission of the armed forces, to seize Belgium by cutting off the Allied forces in that state from France and forcing their quick surrender. To contribute to the grand mission, Hoth pressed his two divisions - 7.Pz.D. and 5.Pz.D. - to cross the Meuse quickly and drive deeply into the defending French forces. With some special insight into the advances required to defeat the Allied forces in Belgium, Hoth pressed his screening corps to match the pace of Kleist's campaign *Schwerpunkt* force of seven mobile divisions, also advancing to cross the Meuse farther south at Sedan. Throughout the advance, Hoth and his forces revealed again and again the speed, flexibility and opportunistic will at the heart of the German Army. They lived their bias for action.

---

39. See in *7.Pz.Div., Ia, Gefechts, 1940, XV. A. K.*, p. 1, U.S. Archives, German Records, Divisions, T-315, Roll 401, Fr. 000619.

Chapter 2

The 7th Panzer Division in the Russian Campaign, June-July 1941

The 7.Pz.D., after all it had accomplished in France, under Hoth and Rommel, faced even greater challenges in Russia. With Rommel's transfer, command of the 7.Pz.D. went to *Generalmajor* von Funck (commander of 5.Pz.R, 5.Pz.D. in France.) Quite astonishingly, the 7.Pz.D., led by Funck, met the greater challenges in Russia with even greater achievements. On the road to Moscow in 1941, the Germans fought three great encirclement battles; in each, 7.Pz.D. closed the northern arm of the envelopment and encircled immense numbers of strategic Soviet Forces. In four short days, 22-25 June 41, 7.Pz.D. would move more than 345 km through the Soviet Union, cutting the main road and rail connection between Minsk and Moscow at Smolevichi, 30 km east of Minsk. Two days later, 17.Pz.D. from the Panzer Group operating farther south would link up near Minsk and close the outer arms of an encirclement that would yield 324,000 prisoners and 3,332 destroyed or captured tanks. Starting to advance eastward again on 3 July 41, 7.Pz.D. would move 365 Km cutting the main road and rail connection between Smolensk and Moscow at Jarcewo, 55 km *east* of Smolensk on 16 July 41. Over the next few days, elements of the Panzer Group operating farther south would link up between Smolensk and Jarcewo and effect an encirclement that would yield 310,000 prisoners and 3,205 tanks. After Hitler's diversion of forces south in the months of August and September 41, 7.Pz.D. would advance again as part of a great offensive launched on 2 October 41. Starting to advance on that day, 7.Pz.D. would reach the northern outskirts of Vyasma 106 hours later and linking up a short time later with I0.Pz.D. to effect the immediate encirclement of 55 Soviet divisions and a following battle that would yield 660,000 prisoners and 1,242 tanks in pockets at Vyasma and further south at Bryansk. The prisoners yielded largely from the pockets noted above totalled *more than 14 times* the number of Rumanian and German prisoners taken from the Stalingrad pocket in January and February 1943.

To add insult to injury, 7.Pz.D. would go on in the later German offensive of 16 November 41, to move another 110 km forward into the Soviet Union from its position on that date and *seize a bridgehead across the Moscow-Volga Canal* at Yachroma on 27 November. 7.Pz.D. would take few prisoners on this last drive and would *not* cut the great road between Moscow and the vast city of Gorki lying to the east. To the bitter end of the German strategic offensive of 1941, however, 7.Pz.D. continued to lead the northern wing of the enveloping German forces. *Generalmajor* Funck led the division to unmatched success in World War II. Somewhere in the experience of the division during that period, there are lessons in operational style, tactical technique, and even weaponry that could be applied to western ground force operations today.

● ● ● ● ●

In Operation Barbarossa, which turned out to be the opening phase of the Russian Campaign, Funck and 7.Pz.D. began the fighting under *General der Panzertruppen* Schmidt in XXXIX.Pz.K.[40] In turn, the Pz.K. lay under Hermann Hoth, now a *Generaloberst* (Colonel General), and commander of Pz.Gr.3 (Panzergruppe 3, or Panzer Group 3). Hoth had put on a formidable performance with XV.A.K.(mot.) in France in sometimes pressing a commander even as aggressive as Rommel. The High Command of the Army recognized Horn's talents as a leader

---

40. By this time in the war the Germans had changed the names of corps headquarters controlling mobile divisions from A.K. (mot.) to Pz.K. *(Panzer Korps).*

of higher level mobile formations; he was considered comparable in many ways to the great Heinz Guderian. The *OKH* selected Hoth & Guderian to lead the Panzer Groups of Army Group Center, the two most important Panzer force commands in the German Army in 1941 (including even the soon to be famous *Afrika Korps* formed that same year). Hoth would display enormous self confidence and aggressiveness in the planning for Barbarossa. He suggested, for example, to his commander, *Generalfeldmarschal* (General Field Marshal) Fedor von Bock, Commander, Army Group Center, that the first encirclement of Soviet forces in the campaign be made just east of Smolensk approximately 640 km straight line distance into the Soviet Union for Pz.Gr.3 and almost 700 km for Guderian's Pz.Gr.2. Funck and 7.Pz.D. would be moving under tough and aggressive commanders in the advance into the Soviet Union.

•　•　•　•　•

7.Pz.D. began the Russian Campaign with an organization similar to that in France. Pz.R.25 under *Oberst* Rothenburg was the key maneuver element and continued to be organized into three Panzer battaltions. Although the Army had formed 10 additional Panzer divisions for the Russian campaign by the ruthless expedient of splitting in half each of the 10 existing divisions at the end of the French Campaign, 7.Pz.D. had a substantial total of 284 light and medium tanks compared with the much smaller number of 170 in France. It remains a bit of a mystery why 7.Pz.D. should have had so many tanks when in principle, it should have had roughly half as many based on the way in which the 10 new divisions had been formed by taking tanks from the older divisions. German tank production remained very thin at this time, many tanks had been lost and worn out in Poland and France and the Balkans, and the feeble *Panzer I* had been almost completely phased out of use. The "trick" perhaps is that 7.Pz.D. would fight the great battles of 1941 with a high percentage (initial outfitting of 167) of the mechanically robust but battle marginal Czech-manufacture 38

(t) tanks weighing only about 11 tons and armed with a high quality but necessarily light 37mm cannon. The division, in effect, would go to war in Russia with a lot of high quality, medium-light battle tanks compensating perhaps for the lack of a stronger battle tank in the 20-ton class like the *Panzer III*.

The remainder of 7.Pz.D. would be concentrated in terms of combat power in S.R.6 and S.R.7 with the former equipped partially with *Schutzen Panzer Wagen* (*SPW* or Armored Personnel Carriers). The division received the first of those vehicles on 1 March 41 and agonized over the tactical employment of troops in them. The Germans faced the question of whether to develop tactics of fighting from the vehicles or deploying out of them and fighting with more conventional infantry tactics. The division used K.7 and Pz.AA.37 as the remaining maneuver elements. The artillery regiment of the division, A.R.78, as a result of the experiences of the French Campaign, was reorganized, having one of its three light (105mm) howitzer battalions replaced by a heavy (150mm) howitzer battalion for the same overall total of three artillery battalions.

The division would continue to have organic 88mm and 20mm *FLAK* in FLA.86 (Army Antiaircraft Gun Detachment 86) and self propelled 105mm heavy infantry guns (special artillery howitzers manned by infantry crews). The division anticipated problems with supply over the primitive, unpaved Russian road system, and the Ib (Quartermaster or Logistics Officer) of the division had paid special attention to the organization of the heavy combat trains (truck columns) carrying fuel. The division continued to have an Army aviation detachment with light fixed-wing aircraft dedicated primarily to reconnaissance (as opposed, for example, to spotting of artillery fire).

As an elite, offensively oriented division with deep, strategic objectives in war, 7.Pz.D. lay approximately 1,200 km from its attack positions for the advance into the Soviet Union for reasons of deception and security until shortly before the outbreak of war. The division began to load troops for the move east from the area around Bonn only at 1000 on 8 June 41. The complexity and challenge of this move was similar in magnitude to the amphibious operations planned and executed by the Allies in Europe and the Pacific. The operations staff had to break up the division into 64 *train loads* complicated by differing types of rolling stock (train carriages) necessary for personnel, motor vehicles, tanks, heavy weapons, bridge columns, etc. The staff also had to arrange train loads of newly allotted, trucks from Ulm, Leipzig, and Paris, France. The trains had to be scheduled to conform to the normal pattern of rail traffic as much as possible and the tanks (all 284 of them) concealed during the movement and especially after arrival in East Russia southeast of Lotzen (Gizyko, Poland) during unloading. Not unlike an amphibious operation, the troop units had to arrive at the right times and adjacent to assembly areas as correct for the move to the border (movement ashore) into tactical positions in which combat would take place. The operations staff of the division, headed by *Major i.G.* Heidkamper was only a small fraction of the size and rank, for example, of a present-day Marine Corps division, whose large staff is partly justified by the "unique" complexities of the amphibious operation. Barbarossa was not a one-time event as a great strategic offensive. German operational staffs faced and solved the problems of similar great movements of forces in Poland, Norway, France, and the Balkans.

By 21 June 41, 7.Pz.D. moved into its tactical assembly areas and assault positons. The division would be supported in the initial assault by a complex array of army artillery detachments, corps artillery, Luftwaffe Flak, and an attached infantry regiment that would advance initially across one half of the front of the division for various tactical reasons. Unlike the brief attachment of the horse-drawn infantry regiment, the division would move into the Soviet Union with attached corps troops that would remain with the division for long periods of time in 1941. The small operations staff of 7.Pz.D., for example would request, receive, and operation- ally control a 100m gun battery, two 150mm guns, one 210mm mortar (*Morser*, or large caliber very short barreled artillery piece), smoke regiment (with 100mm conventional mortars), self-propelled antitank company (47mm AT guns on *Panzer I* chassis) and strong pioneer detachments.

OKH placed the major point of effort in the Russian Campaign with Army Group Center and the concept of a strong attack directly toward Moscow.[41] The Chief of Staff of the German army reasoned that such an attack would keep the German effort focused on a clear physical objective. He also reasoned that the government of the Soviet Union would be forced to commit the main concentration of the Soviet army in the defense of the political, communications, and mobilization center of the state with the accompanying necessary possibility of its destruction. Hitler marched to a different strategic drumbeat that remains ill-understood to the present day. Hitler's diffusion of the German strategic effort toward Leningrad, the Eastern Ukraine, and the Crimea support a view that he was more interested in making certain of the seizure of those objectives than the defeat of the armies defending them. Hitler seems to have had a siege mentality in which he was more interested in establishing effective siege lines for Germany than decisively finishing off the Soviet Union in the war begun by him.

Without Rommel now, but with Rothenburg (Pz.R.25) and Unger (S.R.6) remaining from the French Campaign, the division would have a daring style that would be difficult for the Soviets to manage. Independently of Rommel, the German general staff system had provided the division with a streamlined system of command: except for suggestion and opinion of any senior commander in 7.Pz.D., the division commander made his decisions in brief discussions with only one man in the division - the Ia, or operations officer. The 7.Pz.D. had no assistant division commander and no chief of staff. The division

---

41. *OKH* or *Oberkommando des Heeres* (High Command of the Army).

commander commanded, the Ia attended to the details of staff work, the artillery commander (*Arko*) coordinated fire support. The division that moved out of the edge of darkness into the Soviet Union at 0305 on 22 June 41 was committed to action not to management and discussion.

Just as in France, 7.Pz.D. advanced to cross a major river obstacle, namely, the Nieman River, broad but slow flowing, and 63-68 km distant where two big bridges crossed it in and near Olita (Alytus). Although SR.6 and S.R.7 would make the first assault into the Soviet Union along with I.r.90 (Infantry Regiment 90) on their right,[42] Pz.R.25 would quickly pass through the motorized rifle regiments and with K.7 and Pz.A.A.37 seize the bridge over the Nieman at Olita another 4.5 km farther east at approximately 1245. The latter bridge was not captured as an afterthought. The division used thrust lines as a quick, flexible, and secure technique to locate units and assign missions based on the success of the system in France. The division commander assigned the second thrust line in the war to run from the rail and road intersection 10.5 km east of Kalvarija through one intermediate point and *end on the bridge 4.5 km east of Olita.*[43]

On the first day of the war, the German style in a fluid offensive situation is illustrated by the initiative demanded of the leaders of K.7 and Pz.A.A.37. The division commander, in his written order for the attack, assigned K.7 the *mission-oriented task* "with Pz.Jg.42 to remain at the disposal of the division while reconnoitering as close as possible behind S.Brig.7 or else Pz.R.25 through the towns of Trump alie and Mergutrakiai."[44] The division commander has told

---

42. See these arrangements in, *7.Pz.D., Ia, Anlagen zum Kriegstagebuch Nr. 3, Teil I, 1 Juni-27 September 1941, Anlage zu 7.Pz.Div. Ia Nr. 460/41 g. Kdos. vom 13.6.41*, U.S. Archives, German Records, Divisions, T-315, Roll 406, Fr. 000469. The sketch shows the assembly areas and attack positions for the advance across the Soviet border. The German troops began to move into this position on 20 June 41 (See also Map 4 in appendix).

43. See in, *7.Pz.D., Ia, Anlagen zum Kriegstagebuch Nr. 3, Teil I, 1 Juni-27 September 1941, Anlage 19, Stosslinien, 19.6.41*, U.S., Archives, German Records, Divisions, T-315, Roll 406, Fr. 000503.

44. Ibid., *Anlage 20, Divisionbefehl fur den Angriffe am B-Tag*, 20.6.41, Fr. 000508.

the officer commanding K7 to keep up with the big maneuver force that had the most success in moving along the main axis of advance and be ready to do what the division commander decided depending on actual developments in the war. In the same written order, Funck gave Pz.A.A.37 the task "to hold itself ready after the breakthrough of the narrow trafficable area at Mikaliskiai to move to the front for reconnaissance up to the Nieman River."[45] Funck (and the Ia) wasted few words in assigning tasks, showed confidence in the initiative of the subordinate commanders, and obviously accepted the reality that no plan survives first contact with the enemy.

After the seizure of the two bridges over the Nieman, Pz.R.25 (minus IId Battalion) and K.7 with various supporting forces especially artillery, Flak, and pioneers, had built up the northern bridgehead opposite Olita until struck by a Soviet tank attack. The Germans were not surprised; intelligence at various levels had agreed before the war on the presence of the Soviet 5th Tank Division in the general area of the attack. The Germans were mildly jarred by the scale and intensity of the attacks that continued through approximately 1900 and seem to have been made by a force of about 200 tanks. Pz.R.25 fought a battle in the afternoon that *Oberst* Rothenburg remarked was particularly tough. Rothenburg's tanks "shot up" or captured intact 70 Soviet "medium and heavy" tanks (See Map 5 for the location of Olita).

By approximately 1930, Pz.R.25 could begin preparations to continue the advance, having decisively thrown back the Soviet tanks. By 2130, Funck had pressed much of the division into the two bridgeheads now roughly 70 km from the border, and even Pz.R.21 from the adjacent (to the north) 20.Pz.D. had slipped into the northern bridgehead. The division, in fact, was ready to move - Pz.R.25 out of the northern lodgement slightly in advance of the rest of the division in the southern bridgehead and with 20.Pz.D. screening to the north.

---

45. Ibid., Fr. 000509.

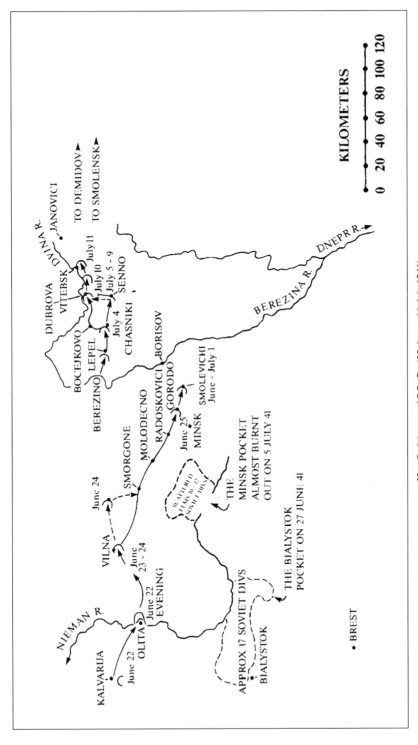

Map 5. Advance of 7.Pz.D., (22 June - 11 July 1941).
The Episode of the Encirclement West of Minsk and Drive to Vitebsk.

59

Neither Schmidt as corps commander nor Funck on his own initiative got the advance going again until 0900 the next morning (23 June 41). Significant opportunity eluded the Germans here, for example, the possibility of getting to Vilna with greater disruption of Soviet command and control and overrunning and scattering of reserves. The question arises: why did Funck not move the division?

The answer is both interesting and instructive. The Ia made the cryptic comment at the end of the entries in his log for 22 June 40 that further attack with Pz.R.25 was only possible with the accomplishment of refueling and resupply of ammunition.[46] The Ib of the division goes into more detail on the course of events in his diary. He makes it clear that in spite of the months of preparation for Barbarossa in 9th Army (9.A.O.K.), Pz.Gr.3, XXXIX.Pz.K. and for a shorter period of time in 7.Pz.D., the gigantic surge of the German army and Luftwaffe ground units across the border overloaded the road system and blocked the movement forward of the fuel and ammunition columns of the division supply service. As early as 0530 on 22 June 41, the Ia ordered two heavy columns of fuel and one light column of ammunition forward for Pz.R.25. Both the Ia and Ib personally intervened to get the fuel and ammunition forward. They were both successful and they were only able to get the supplies to the Panzer regiment and rest of the division around Olita approximately *24 hours late* in the early morning of 23 June 41. In essence, Pz.R.25 and the other combat elements of 7.Pz.D. moved forward with no traffic problems except perhaps for approximately 200 tanks of the Soviet 5th Tank Division while the columns of the division trains inched forward in German traffic. 7.Pz.D. learned from this experience and, in a potential lesson for operations today, *included fuel and ammunition columns in and among the forward combat elements* in future prepared offensives in which large numbers of troops were concentrated in advance for a major attack.

---

46. See in *7.Pz.D., Ia, Kriegstagebuch Nr. 3 (Fuhrungsabteil-ung), Einsatz Sowjetrussland, 22.6.41*, U.S., Archives, German Records, Divisions, T-315, Roll 406, Fr. 000014.

At 0900 23 June 41, the mass of the division advanced eastward then northeastward to skirt the southern edge of the great city of Vilna and the heights east of it, the latter approximately 40 km distant. Both Schmidt and Funck agreed that 7.Pz.D. as a mobile formation should not get involved in a fight for a big city like Vilna but move close enough to secure the road net around it for a continuation of the advance toward Minsk. They also felt that the Germans on the outskirts so quickly in the war might cause the Soviets to evacuate the town without turning it into a fortress. Funck sent out Pz.AA.37 as the advanced detachment of the division and placed Pz.R.25 as the leading element of the mass of the division following behind the armored cars and motorcycles of the reconnaissance battalion. After "hard fighting" in several places along the way and one significant river crossing, Pz.R.25 reached "the heights" east of Vilna at 1900 23 June 41. Funck, who had stationed himself forward with Pz.R.25, ordered the rest of the division to close up just south of Vilna and behind the tanks of the Panzer regiment. The rest of the division moved into that area from 2300-0200 while under attack by Soviet tanks units which attacked the German march columns destroying "individual vehicles." The potential danger of the German position is illustrated by the fact that in the next two days units of 20. and 7.Pz.D. would put out of action *80 Soviet tanks* in the area 7.Pz.D. had marched through the previous evening.

The division spent 24 June 41 tidying up around Vilna and preparing for another leap forward on the following day. K.7, which seized 25 intact aircraft on Vilna-South Airport at 0615, advanced into Vilna against a quickly disappearing enemy and had taken the city by 0840. Funck then ordered a strong reconnaissance force directly east while beginning to concentrate the mass of the division - Pz.R.25, S.R.6, S.R.7 and A.R.78 - southeast of Vilna for the anticipated order by corps headquarters to advance through the big rail center at Molodecno north of Minsk. Funck sent the warning order to S.R.6 and S.R.7 at 1700 to concentrate southeast of Vilna but faced the dilemma that at that time the so-called large fuel columns of the division that carried fuel for the motorized infantry had been held up and only Pz.R.25 had enough fuel to continue the advance. Funck confronted the question of whether to continue the advance with Pz.R.25 alone or keep the division concentrated but not moving while waiting for the fuel. In the actual event, corps headquarters did not send down the order to continue the advance until after midnight 24 June 41, and Funck was able to refuel the motorized infantry regiments for an advance on the morning of 25 June 41. Funck *also* on 24 June 41 ordered I./Pz.R.25 and Pz.A.A.37 directly east 60 km from Vilna to seize a bridgehead over the Vilija River either as part of the main route of advance of 7.Pz.D. *or* to turn over to the somewhat slower moving 20.Pz.D. immediately adjacent to the left.

Funck reinforced S.R.6 and set it out at 0900 25 June 40 as a powerful advanced detachment toward Molodecno, which was a substantial 100 km east. In a noteworthy performance, the spearhead of S.R.6 reached Molodecno at 1715 and went on into the evening to "seize and hold" the heights beyond Radoskovici a total of 145 km from the starting point of S.R.6 earlier on the same day. Operating as lead element of the mass of the division, Pz.R.25 moved closely behind S.R.6 during the entire day putting out of action numerous Soviet tanks and armored reconnaissance vehicles along the road. By 1915, Pz.R.25 lay 10 km southeast of Molodecno and continued forward to move through the position of S.R.6 beyond to the vicinity of Maki near the Minsk-Moscow "autobahn", an advance of approximately 170 km straight line distance for the day. The figure is a dramatic one showing 7.Pz.D. having exploded forward before the end of the fourth day of fighting in the east to a position *between* Minsk and Moscow (See Map 5).

Funck stationed himself and the division operations staff with Pz.R.25 during this dramatic advance and set up *the division command post* during the evening of 25 June 41 4 km southeast of Radoskovici only 29 km from the capital of White Russia. Funck also moved forward K.7 and Pz.A.A.37 the latter all the way from its mission in the sector of 20.Pz.D. By midnight on 25 June 41, Funck had concentrated the mass of 7.Pz.D. north and east of Minsk. Funck lay with a powerful force in terms of its demonstrated combat power now far to the rear of three Soviet armies fighting in the area between Bialystok and Novogrodek with approximately 500,000 men. The next day, Funck would edge his division farther to the southeast and cut the autobahn and main rail connection between that Soviet force and Moscow. Almost incredibly, 7.Pz.D. lay approximately 150 km east of the center of mass of the Soviet armies defending White Russia.

The following day, 26 June 41, after an unexplained pause in operations for the entire morning, Funck issued orders for the continuation of the advance and moved the division forward starting at 1600. Pz.R.25 led the advance and cut the main rail line and road between Minsk and Moscow near Sloboda 25 km *east* of Minsk at approximately 2200. Pz.R.25 and the accompanying S.R.6 continued to fight against sporadic Soviet resistance. The Germans encountered a newly constructed "autobahn" not shown on their maps and lying just to the north of the older one between Minsk and Moscow. The discovery of this great road caused some confusion, but Pz.R.25 signalled to division still during darkness: "victory along the entire line." Unfortunately for the Germans, *Oberst* Rothenburg was badly wounded and would be killed in action the following day while being evacuated in an ambulance along dangerous roads back toward Vilna - shot dead by Russian infantry along the route. Unfortunately for the Russians, Pz.R.25 would surprise and destroy two "disoriented" trains on the rail line to Moscow during the evening and put out of action 20 Russian tanks in later action. By midnight of 26 June 41, Funck had placed 7.Pz.D. astride the main communications line between Minsk and Moscow and by the next morning would have the division in different positions along that line between Sloboda and Smolensk (15 km farther *east*) and then curving north to block

Soviet attacks from the direction of Moscow. Funck, in effect, set up on 26-27 June 51, a large German defensive perimeter northeast of Minsk that blocked Soviet escape from the west and reinforcement from the east.

How is it possible that such a situation had come to pass? More specifically, how were the Germans able to advance 170 km with the division mass comprising Pz.R.25, S.R.6, K.7, Pz.A.A.37 and most of A.R.78 into an area so important to the Soviets in the brief period from 0900 through approximately midnight 25 June 41? Also specifically, how were the Germans able to resupply themselves in so extreme a position? The answer is that 7.Pz.D. advanced and resupplied itself by using the flexibility, initiative, and rapid tempo that characterized their performance. Funck, for example, knew by the evening of 24 June 41 that Pz.Gr.3 was about to turn approximately 90 degrees to the southeast and effect the encirclement of the Soviets in White Russia. Funck was simultaneously ready for but uneasy about this move. The division had been at Vilna one day too long and he was ready to go. S.R.7 - one half of his motorized infantry - however, was tied up in securing the area south of Vilna and Pz.A.A.37 on his own orders had been sent 60 km east in prudent but misplaced anticipation of operations in that direction. Funck was also uneasy about the supply situation which remained dislocated by the traffic overload of the initial surge over the border. When it became apparent at midnight on 24 June 41 that his division was to advance in the morning as the extreme forward and outside wing of the encirclement of the Soviets from the north, Funck knew that accelerating the tempo of the attack was more important than waiting for the whole division to be concentrated or allowing a marginal supply situation to dictate a halt.

S.R.6 led the advance moving boldly in the style of the attack in France: in meeting engagements "all barrels" would be fired in the direction of the enemy to bowl him over and continue the advance;

one-word oral orders characterized brief deployments from movement in column to roust out small but tough and well placed enemy units that could not be bypassed or reduced to immediate flight; the long-barreled 100mm guns of A.R.78 (attached from corps) were placed well forward where they could fire at distant ranges in front of S.R.6 to stimulate panic, confusion, and flight among Russians caught completely off guard because of their assumed safe distance from the front. The division commander placed Pz.R.25 behind S.R.6 because of the observed Russian practice of attacking with tanks against the rear elements of advancing German columns. Placed far enough back to be out of sight of the attacking Soviets, Pz.R.25 several times came to the assistance of the last battalion in the advancing column of S.R.6 to advance with particular boldness because the motorized infantry had no fear of being "cut off" by the Soviet tanks with Pz.R.25 following.

The more detailed accounts of the advance of S.R.6 give additional insights into the German offensive style.[47] The operations detachment of the regiment recorded the events of the advance in a barely preserved account that shows S.R.6 being ordered to put together an advanced detachment at 0700 and begin the attack southeast into White Russia by 0900. Because of supply difficulties, however, the following remarkable situation developed that shows the Germans at a peak of self confidence and urgency in the advance. Quite amazingly, the mass of S.R.6 that was to follow had only enough fuel to march at most approximately 40 km, i.e., nowhere near the distance to its assigned operational objective, just north of Minsk. It is difficult to imagine what the Germans realistically had in mind here but it is clear that they trusted in some special war fighting star and the opportunity associated with action in war. Funck essentially was more willing to advance 40 km until the S.R.6 fuel supplies ran out and trust to some

---

47.   *7.Pz.D, Ia, Tagesmeldungen. 20. Juni-10, 1941, Schutzen-Regiment 6, Abt. Ia, 27.6.41, Morgenmeldung fur die Zeit vom 25.6.41, 09.00 Uhr bis 27.6.41, 01.00 Uhr,* U.S. Archives, German Records, Divisions, T-315, Roll 407, Fr. 000889-000893.

opportunity to keep things going than to sit in position and wait tamely for resupply. At this point the story becomes even more unlikely, because, "at the last minute a (Soviet) fuel dump was discovered"[48] and the mass of S.R.6 quickly fueled and sent off after its advanced detachment.

Funck provided a lesson for energetic leaders of mobile divisions by placing himself at the head of Pz.R.25 and just behind the mass of S.R.6 where he could exert his will. When the advanced detachment of S.R.6 reached Smorgone approximately 65 km from its assembly area near Vilna, the point company headed directly south along a route of advance that would have led it into Minsk directly from the west - a terrible error. At the right location, up front with the division in war, "directly as the battalion with the point company turned off toward Losk"[49] to the south, the division commander "personally" moved forward and gave the veteran regimental commander the order to move in the correct, decisive direction toward Molodecno to the southeast.

The German success of this day, however, is not explained adequately in any of the observations above. A key, possibly the key, to this front shattering advance comes in the following disarmingly succinct and matter of fact comment on the advance: Especially in built-up areas, through attack by fire, the enemy sought to break up the advance of the columns a result, however, which he did not achieve.[50]

This statement presents an operational picture of S.R.6 advancing with little conventional regard for heavy fire directed against its columns on the road. The subtlety in the situation was that the Germans had as high a regard as any troops for fire directed against them but refused

---

48. Ibid., Fr. 000889.
49. Ibid., Fr. 000889.
50. Ibid., Fr. 000890.

in every case, except for a tank attack before Smorgone that *physically* overran part of 7./II./S.R.6 and the regimental motorcycle platoon, to deploy and attack the Soviets. Toward, the end of the day, 3 km west of Radoskovici (about 127 km along the route of advance since morning), the advanced elements of S.R.6 overran a strong Soviet column moving on the same road in the opposite direction. "Through immediate setting to work," the German units destroyed Soviet trucks and tanks on the road and captured a significant number of 152mm long barreled guns of an artillery unit. The energy and style of the 7.Pz.D. is illustrated by the motorized riflemen in this engagement neither collecting nor securing these valuable weapons but simply disabling them where they were scattered along the road.

Funck had confronted severe fuel and ammunition problems on 22 and 23 June 41 but on 25 June discovered an enormous Soviet fuel depot intact in Vilna. The division Supply Service had begun to function more effectively as traffic thinned out on the roads, but the Soviet fuel depot would shorten the haul distances for the German truck columns carrying fuel during the next few days. The Germans would still have to haul ammunition from farther back at Varena 67 km southwest of Vilna but would survive that situation as the dumps moved forward. The divisions confronted a supply crisis again, however, on the evening of 25 June 41 because of the 170 km leap forward. Large numbers of partly dispersed but dangerous Soviet infantry and even manned armored vehicles still lay along the route of advance. The situation was disastrous along the approximately 70 km of road from Molodecno eastward to the area behind the mass of the division fighting by midnight 26 June 41 in the area around Smolevichi.

On 27 June 41, a supply crisis fell on the division. Although the Germans were moving fuel and ammunition forward into army-level dumps at reasonable distances behind the fighting fronts and had captured large Soviet fuel supplies in Vilna and Molodecno, 7.Pz.D.

was unable to move the supply columns of the division supply service along the road from Molodecno through Gorodok to the defenses centered around Smolevici. During the morning, Ib (the division Quartermaster) pleaded with the Ia to set up an "escort system" for the truck supply columns. Ia maintained that no troops could be spared from the perimeter to establish such a system, and Ib at 1400 informed the division command post that fuel and ammunition would be delayed at least until the next morning because of the projected destruction of the columns, bad road conditions worsened by rain during the day, etc. The Ia was adamant, however, and around 1700 ordered Ib to move the columns beginning not later than 2200 that evening - Soviet infantry, tanks, rain, and sandy rutted roads notwithstanding. Ib personally stationed himself along the road after 1700; he observed parts of *Nebelregiment 51* (Nebel.51, or 51st Smoke Regiment armed with 100mm mortars) moving forward, and using impeccable initiative, he searched out the regimental commander and convinced him to provide security for the supply columns.[51] The result: the columns reached Macki close enough to the fighting for the combat troops to pick up the fuel and ammunition, thus allowing division to narrowly overcome another supply crisis caused by its speed in the offense.

On 28 June 41, the division faced another supply crisis as the Ib could not move the supply columns along the road from Gorodok through Macki closer to the front at Smolevici. The Ib lost the support of Nebel.51 as it went into combat and was not able to get support opportunistically from 20.Pz.D. which had moved up alongside of 7.Pz.D. and had begun to share the road with his division. On the morning of 29 June 41, the Ib received word from *Leutnant* Freese in Pz.R.25 that *Oberst* Rothenburg had been killed while being evacuated along the dangerous stretch of supply road. At that moment, the

---

51. See this in, *7.Pz.D., Ib, kriegstagebuch der Quartiermeister-Abteilung, 27. Juni 1941*, U.S., Archives, German Records, Divisions, T-315, Roll 423, Fr. 000024.

Ib, *Major i.G.* Liese simply ordered Freese to assemble an escort force and bring forward supply columns from Gorodok. By 1400, the columns were moving along the roads effectively without loss. At 1400, the Ia under the impact of the death of Rothenburg, ordered the forming of a strong escort force to keep the road open; Pz.R.25 sent 10 tanks in a small task force under *Oberleutnant* Albrecht to escort supplies as required and the crisis finally passed - helped also by the arrival of powerful additional German forces closing in to complete the destruction of the Soviet forces in the great pockets west of Minsk.

The following situation characterizes the necessarily chaotic combat and supply situation in and amongst 7.Pz.D. as it arrived deep in the rear of strategic-level Soviet forces. On 27 June 41, *Leichte Flak-Abteilung 84* I.Flak 84, or 84th Light Antiaircraft Gun Detachment lay along the route of advance of 7.Pz.D. and attached to it for antiaircraft defense of the road. At 1100, I.Flak 84 engaged eight Soviet SB-2, two-engined medium bombers attacking German units moving on the road near Gorodek. The Flak detachment, armed with 20mm automatic cannons observed the crashes of two Soviet aircraft hit at low altitude by high explosive (HE) projectiles. Three hours later, I.Flak 84 came under attack by 10 more Soviet bombers while defending the 7.Pz.D. road and this time drove them off by putting up heavy fire from all guns that prevented the attacking aircraft from making bombing runs. Then, at 1600 the Flak detachment received word that fuel and ammunition columns of the division along the main road forward from Gorodek, i.e., in among the division and its defensive "perimeter," were under attack by Soviet troops with machine guns and anti- tank cannons. The Flak detachment moved 2./I.Flak 84 with six 20mm cannons to engage the enemy in the "middle" of the division defensive area and save the supply columns. The detachment attacked vigorously with its automatic cannons suppressing the fire, driving off the enemy and even putting out of action several lightly armored Soviet tanks with armor piercing ammunition. This action illustrates the uncertainty and chaos of the operational situation and the real dangers posed to the division supply columns.

In the period 25-27 June 41, 7.Pz.D. placed its units astride the main Soviet line of communications to the armies fighting in White Russia and successfully defended itself against all efforts of the Soviets to escape to the east or break in from the west. On the latter day, 17.Pz.D. arrived from the south and completed the cutting of *all* ground communications to the vast Soviet forces west of Minsk from the rest of the Soviet Union. The powerful German 4th and 9th Infantry Armies *(9. Armee and 4. Armee)* surged forward and by 27 June had encircled approximately 17 Soviet divisions in a pocket whose *eastern* edge lay *200 km west of Minsk.* On that day, the pocket would be 30 km wide and 130 km long and the Germans would soon take approximately 170,000 prisoners out of it. The Soviets would get large numbers of troops away from this area but the bulk of them would be caught in the great outer arms of the encirclement set by 7. and 17.Pz.Divs. east of Minsk, and soon manned by the hard marching German infantry divisions and a small number of mobile divisions. By 5 July 41, the remnants of an additional 10-12 Soviet divisions would lie close to surrender in a great pocket 50 km wide and 70 km long that would give up approximately 150,000 prisoners in the area west and southwest of Minsk.

Days earlier, however, on 29 June 41, XXXDCPz.K. would alert 7.Pz.D. for a concentration of its units farther east for a continuation of the offensive toward Moscow. At 0935, Headquarters, XXXDCPz.K somewhat ominously warned the division that "the mission for the movement forward to Borisov remained standing, the time still to be ordered."[52] The next day, 30 June 41, Pz.R.25 reported to division that it had the considerable number of 149 tanks, mostly robust but lightly

---

52. *7.Pz.D., Ia, Kriegstagebuch Nr. 3, 29.6.41,* U.S. Archives, German Records, Divisions T-315, Roll 406, Fr. 000024.

armed *Panzer 38(t)* tanks, ready for another major offensive. Later in the day, Funck ordered the commander of K.7 reinforced by tanks artillery, pioneers, and antitank guns to move out to the north and east of the existing location of the divisions still near Smolevici east of Minsk. The Germans had a special genius for putting together specially tailored *Kampfgruppen* (battle groups) that was an important part of their style in war. During the strategic offensives of 1939-1941, the Germans constructed their mobile advances out of the fire and maneuvers of continually changing battle groups. The German way in war could be likened to the continuous formation of combat groups each with its own mission oriented task, resultant combat, and reformation into yet another combat group for the next task. Here perhaps we have a valuable clue for how to practice war during peacetime: instead of practicing set piece advances, we might be better served to task our officers to put together "ad hoc" battle groups to master the sudden danger of enemy counterattack and to take advantage of the fleeting opportunity characteristic of so many situations on the offensive.

At 1200 on 1 July 41, Headquarters, XXXIX.Pz.K. gave the division the new mission to put together an advanced detachment *(Vorausabteilung)* consisting specifically of one motorized infantry battalion, one Panzer detachment, one pioneer battalion, and one artillery battalion. Corps headquarters directed the division to have this advanced detachment ready to move toward Lepel 100 km north northeast of Smolevici but with the specific route of advance left open for the flexibility of corps in making the final decision. The division, in effect, had been told to be ready to move off immediately but not told which of several possible routes of advance it would be required to take. Funck knew that big things were pending when the Commanding General of VIII. Air Corps, the Baron von Richthofen, arrived at 1400 at the division command post to coordinate liaison and support for the new offensive. At 1500, *Generaloberst* Hoth, Commander, Pz.Gr.3 (i.e., the next echelon of command *above* corps) visited 7.Pz.D. and oriented Funck on the general picture for the entire offensive. Hoth gave Funck the mission oriented order to get to Lepel by a successful surprise attack across the Beresim River directly from the west *but*, if such a coup de main were not possible, to shift the advance farther south to another crossing site.

On 2 July 41, the mass of the division moved north from the area around Smolevici and the next morning, 3 July, advanced directly from the west toward Lepel across the bridge at Beresino on the Beresina River. At 1037, Pz.R.25 arrived at the bridge over the Ulla River at Lepel and by 1400 the Ia of the division had set up the division command post only 3 km to the west of the city. By late evening, 7.Pz.D. had placed the division in assembly areas along the Ulla River ready for the advance across the river at Lepel and the advance directly east towards Vitebsk 100 km farther east.

The general strategic picture was a dramatic one at this time in the war. At the highest level, Adolf Hitler, who was vacillating wildly among different objectives for the German Army had made the right decision to continue the march toward Moscow rather than veer off to the north (Leningrad) or south (Don Basin). The army, accordingly, set the great strategic target of the smashing of the Soviet defenses being erected along the Divina and Dnepr Rivers and especially those on the land bridge between the rivers and west of Smolensk. Army Group Center assigned Pz.Gp.3 the task to swing to the north, break up the Soviet defense along the Dvina River, take Vitebsk, and drive into the heights of Jarcewo northeast of Smolensk to cut the "autobahn" and main rail line to that city from Moscow. Pz.Gr.3 assigned XXXDCPz.K. the mission to advance through Lepel, seize Vitebsk and advance to Jarcewo. The corps commander gave Funck the mission to make the initial seizure of Lepel, to drive directly at Vitebsk south of the Dvina River, and then, staying well to the north of the Minsk-Smolensk-Moscow "autobahn," to cut the road in the vicinity of Jarcewo. If this could be done in a timely fashion, the Germans would succeed again in encircling about 500,000 Russians still lying *west* of them.

On the early morning of 4 July 41, the divisions completed the crossing of the Ulla River at Lepel but stood frozen in its advance directly at Vitebsk. In spite of effective planning by the staff and impressive will on the part of the commanders, the division had lost most of its operational mobility due to fuel shortage. The Ia noted earlier, for example, at 2300 on 3 July 41 that the "action radius" of the division had fallen to only 50 km for various individual units. He noted again at 0400 on 4 July 41 that still no fuel had been received and that the mass of the division would be able to advance only after receipt of gasoline. With some coolness and flexibility, the division commander, nevertheless, put together yet another advanced detachment with fuel as available to advance 37 km farther east to Chasniki. The supply service fuel columns continued to be held up by damaged bridges and unpaved sandy roads with inadequate foundations, and fuel did not become available until approximately 1800 in Lepel.

Funck showed originality and decisiveness in putting together the advanced detachment because he assigned the commander of A.R.78, his artillery chief and fire support coordinator to lead the detachment. The following list of units comprising the advanced detachment illustrates the flexibility of the Germans in keeping things moving in the advance:

7.Pz.D. Advanced Detachment (0300 4 July 41)
Commander: Commanding Officer of Div Artillery Regiment

Units: 1 Battalion S.R.6
         1 Platoon 2./PL58
         1 Platoon 2./Pz Jg.42
         1 Platoon 88 mm Flak

         1 Company, Pz.R.25
         2 Batteries I./A.R.78
         1 Battery Nbl.Rgt.51

Funck gave *Oberst* Frolich (Commander, A.R.78) the mission to seize the bridge at Chasniki and, limited only by fuel, continue the advance towards Vitebsk. Funck specifically noted that the mission of holding open the crossing site was that of the following elements of the division; i.e., the advanced detachment was to continue to advance whether or not the enemy pulled himself together to attack the crossing site.

After the road, bridge, and fuel problems of the previous day, Funck got the division going again on the early morning of 5 July 41. The division advanced along two axes with Pz.A.A.37 leading the advanced detachment through Chasniki and Bocejkova toward the narrows a Dubrova between the Dvina River and lakes to the south. K.7 (reinforced) advanced on a separate axis through Chasniki and Senno toward the same narrows at Dubrova. By the evening of 5 July at about midnight, the division stood with the mass of its units on the south bank of the Dvina River at Dubrova only 25 km from the outskirts of Vitebsk. Funck had led 7.Pz.D. well into the land bridge between the Dvina River to the north and the Dnepr to the south. The Soviets, although falling behind in the mobilization process, had managed to concentrate powerful forces almost exactly where 7.Pz.D. now lay.

By 0300 6 July 41 the division units in the Dubrova area were under heavy attack from strong Soviet forces to the east and south-east. Pz.A.A.37 at the forefront of the developing battle informed division headquarters at 0830 that it was "questionable" that the advanced positions could be held. Funck ordered the reconnaissance battalion to hold those positions and moved up III./Pz.R.25 to its assistance and quickly built up yet another battle group designated *Kampfgruppe Thomale* to take over defense of the Dubrova narrows. In the meantime the division battle group based on K.7 farther south had reached Senno at 1030 and a great battle began to develop from that city to the Dvina River along a "front" of about 33 km. By 1230 all of the forward units of the division reported combat with the Soviets. Later in the afternoon after 1430, Funck organized two additional battle groups designated *Kampfgruppen von Boineburg* and *von Unger* alongside and to the rear respectively of *Kampfgruppe Thomale* near the Dubrova narrows. With reinforced K.7, also engaged at Senno, Funck conducted the escalating engagement with four battle groups. By 1440 6 July 41, all of the attached heavy artillery was firing in support of the division which found itself everywhere on the defensive. The artillery held by the division would prove particularly effective in disrupting and scattering Soviet tank units assembling for attack - at 2000, for example, German artillery fire as observed through artillery observation aircraft would "shoot up in flames" seven Soviet tanks in one assembly area.[53] A Soviet prisoner, Captain Logwinoff, 220th Motorized Rifle Division, engaged in the fighting at Vitebsk, would note specifically that the 10 tanks of the division still running after a long march to Vitebsk would all be destroyed by German *Pak* and artillery fire.[54]

On 7 and 8 July 41, Funck engaged powerful enemy forces largely from the newly inserted Soviet 19th Army that included one mechanized and three tank divisions. *Kampfgruppe von Boineburg* and *Kampfgruppe Thomale* bore the brunt of the fighting against Soviet forces that included large numbers of tanks. The severity of the fighting is illustrated by the following data. On 7 July 41, the division put out of action 103 Soviet tanks including six heavy vehicles (2 KV-2 and 4 T-34). The Germans with characteristic candor claimed the destruction of only 20 Soviet trucks and one antitank gun, while they noted that the numbers for tanks and trucks did *not* include vehicles put out of action through artillery fire into assembly areas - a major tactic of the Germans in the battle. German records show the following losses for the same day:

---

53. See, for example, *7.Pz.D., Ia, Kriegstagebuch Nr.3, 6.7.41*, U.S., Archives, German Records, T-315, Roll 406, Fr. 000037.

54. See, *7.Pz.D., Ic, Tatigkeitsbericht, Anlagen zum 1. Abschnitt, Vernehmung Hauptmann Logwinoff, c. 25.7.41*, U.S. Archives, German Records, Divisions, T-315, Roll 426, Fr. 001056.

Final Outcome, Tank Battle, 7 July 41[55]		
	Soviet Losses	**German Losses**[56]
Tanks:	2 KV-2 52-ton 4 T-34 26-ton 98 mostly BT-5, 7 c. 11-14 t	*s.I.G.* (150mm): 1 *l.I.G.* (75 mm): 1
Guns:	3 observed destroyed	Flak 88mm: 2
Trucks:	50 (the Soviets deployed with tanks supported by truck borne troops)	*Pak* 50mm: 1
Personnel:	No Estimate	30 KIA, 100 WIA, 6 MIA

The data show that 7.Pz.D. had a clear - indeed, crushing - tactical superiority over the Soviets. The German loss in tanks, for example, was an *almost* incredibly low two vehicles for an exchange ratio in tanks of more than 50 to 1. This statistic cannot be explained in terms of just German superiority in tank-versus-tank and tank unit-versus-tank unit superiority in tank battles. It also cannot be explained just in terms of the Germans holding on to the battle area and quickly repairing their own lightly damaged but, for example, immobilized tanks. *Hauptmann* Schulz commanding one tank battalion of Pz.R.25 in the Dubrova narrows did succeed, however, in taking the attacking Soviet force "in the flank" (as stated with division-level generality) thereby putting out of action 25 Soviet tanks without a loss to his battalion. The Germans lost during the day two of their precious, heavy 88mm Flak which must have been pressed far forward in the ground battle to have been lost while probably giving a good account of themselves against the Soviet tanks. The German 37mm *Pak* which was useless against the Soviet heavy tanks was capable of destroying the lighter BT-5 and 7 vehicles and probably accounted for a significant number of kills. The German personnel casualties speak for themselves. The Germans suffered

---

55. *7.Pz.D., Ia, Anlagen zum Kriegstagebuch Nr. 3, Teil I, Abschlussergebnis der Panzerkampfe am 7.7.41*, U.S., Archives, German Records, Divisions, T-315, Roll 406, Fr. 000574-000575.

56. *s.I.G.* or heavy infantry gun; *l.I.G.* or light infantry gun.

heavy casualties, claimed no prisoners, and gave no estimates of Soviet losses. The question of the number of Soviets killed by the Germans in such a battle is both intriguing and important. It must be suspected that Soviet losses killed in a battle like this one were catastrophic perhaps as high as 15 times the number of Germans.

The Soviets tended to be frustrated by the tactical damage that they were taking and committed numerous atrocities against the small number of German prisoners that came into their hands. This tactical frustration was compounded by the Soviet policy of claiming to their troops that the Germans shot all prisoners, "skinned them alive," etc. The Russians and other nationalities tended to accept the Soviet claims as literal truth and as a result often fought to the death in hopeless tactical situations. On the other hand, as the Germans dropped *thousands* of surrender leaflets from the air, the Soviet troops discovered the possibility of survival through desertion and surrender after reasonable resistance notwithstanding the danger of being shot by *their own* officers and commissars. The Russians and others surrendered eventually in gigantic numbers in 1941 - the Germans took approximately 3.1 million prisoners from 22 June-17 October 41. When under the control of their own leaders, however, they tended to be edgy, unpredictable, and brutal in the treatment of German prisoners. The German experience brings up the question of how do leaders prepare and instruct their men in combat against such an enemy.

In the tough fighting of 7.Pz.D. on 7 July 41, the following combat action illustrates the toughness of the fighting, the unnecessary, indeed self defeating brutality of the Russians. *Obergefreiter* (Lance Corporal) Hans Steinert in 4./Pz.A.A.37 near Senno at 0430 came under fire in the truck in which he was "moving forward."[57] He and three other

---

57. See this account in, *7.Pz.D., Ic, Tatigkeitsbericht, Russland I, Anlagen Zum I. Abschnitt, Vernehmung, O.-Gefr. Steinert, 8.7.41*, U.S., Archives, German Records, Divisions, T-315, Roll 436, Fr. 001147.

soldiers leaped from the vehicle and returned the fire while the truck turned around and moved back not realizing that four men had been left behind. Two of the Germans were badly wounded a distance away from Steinert, who lay with a leg wound a few meters away from a nearer companion with a light hand wound. Steinert observed several Russian soldiers move past the two severely wounded Germans and shoot each one twice in the head with pistol fire at a range of about one meter. One Russian now close to Steinert shot his lightly wounded comrade twice in the head and then approached him. Steinert played as if he had been killed; the Russian, nevertheless, shot him twice in the head with a pistol, but in a modest combat miracle both pistol rounds failed to penetrate his helmet. Such incidents were commonly reported among the captured then rescued German troops of 7.Pz.D. in the fluid offensive combat of the period. The situation suggests the requirement for systematic behavior on the part of troops overrun and tough discipline to prevent retaliation.

After the violent battles of 7, 8 June 41, 7.Pz.D. began to move east again. Funck alerted the commander of K.7 and the chief (the Germans referred to leaders of units below those designated battalion as *Chef* or chief) of Pz.A.A.37 at 1315 9 July 41 that he was going to put them together as an advanced detachment to move directly east from Senno. By 1440, K.7 had already sent out a reconnaissance troop 14 km east to Kobali that reported no Soviets along the road. The troop reported a startling finding, though, of 20 Soviet tanks which had come under Stuka attack and had been abandoned by their crews under the assumption that the tanks had been put out of action. The German motorcyclists discovered the tanks to be "undamaged" and destroyed every one of them. Later in the afternoon, at 1830, the advanced detachment itself set out against the enemy vacuum to the east. At 1930, Schmidt as commander, XXXIX. Pz.K., somewhat excitedly, ordered the entire division to move out *immediately* to take advantage of the shaken and outpaced Soviets. Schmidt gave Funck the specific task to seize Vitebsk from the south (20.Pz.D. and 20.1.D. (mot.)

would attack from north of the Dvina River) and advance as quickly as possible through Demidov toward Jarcewo *east* of Smolensk.

During the next several days of 10-15 July 41, 7.Pz.D. would move with superlative offensive style. When the division launched coordinated attacks on 10 July 41 in the Dubrova narrows and the area immediately to the south, it still faced an advance of more than 195 km to Jarcewo against a Soviet opponent awakening to the realization that the central front before Moscow was about to collapse. Yet five days later, 7.Pz.D. stood on the "autobahn" *between* Smolensk and Moscow blocking Soviet columns moving east and west and posing a fatal operational threat to all Soviet forces lying to the west of it. When Pz.R.25 faced strong resistance south of the narrows, Funck showed great flexibility by ordering it to break off its attack, move laterally along the front and follow S.R.7 which in the meantime had been making good progress directly through the narrows since 0350 that morning. Later in the day at 1100, based on a major operational rearrangement of forces in Pz.Gr.3, Funck ordered the K.7 *Kampfgruppe* moving east beyond Senno to halt, turn about, move laterally along the front and move in behind Pz.R.25 through the Dubrova narrows. Coming from the liens of encirclement of the pocket at Minsk were on a single day on 2 July 41 it had taken 30,000 Soviet prisoners, 12.Pz.D. moved up as the right hand neighbor of 7.Pz.D. to pin down powerful, dangerous Soviet forces continuing to build up west of Smolensk.

By 1100 11 July 41, Pz.R.25 had reached the southeast outskirts of Vietbsk and engaged in heavy fighting against strong Soviet forces including tanks and artillery. Funck reinforced the tank regiment with an additional battery of Flak to be used in the fight against the Soviet tanks. By evening of the same day, Funck had concentrated the mass of the division immediately south of Vietbsk and was preparing to move directly east through Demidov 85 km distant. During the early hours between 0100 and 0335 12 July 41, Funck began to move the division east and east southeast from Vitebsk. At 0440, the division army aviation detachment reported *100 Soviet tanks* marching in from the southeast toward Vietbsk and only about 18 km away. An extraordinary strategic situation was beginning to develop in which the Soviet high command in the area opposite German Army Group Center was committing powerful forces to regain Vitebsk from the south and defend the Smolensk land bridge well to the *west* of Smolensk. At the very same moment, 7.Pz.D. was heading east away from Vietbsk to seize the distant target of Jarcewo. The situation was as bizarre as one is likely to find in war: German troops of 7.Pz.D. advancing with two other mobile divisions from Vitebsk, east toward Jarcewo while immediately to the south, strategic level Soviet forces were marching west to take Vitebsk. One high command had to be out of touch with strategic reality.

By 13 July 41, Funck and 7.Pz.D. had begun to give evidence of the tempo and sense of urgency that characterized the drive in France from Dinant to Arras (13-21 May 40) and the breathtaking pace of 25 June 41 to Vilna to beyond Minsk. As the tanks of Pz.R.25 rolled (*rollt Pz. Rqt. 25*: uncharacteristically dramatic entry in War Diary) at 0000 on 13 July, Funck put himself and the operations staff with that regiment. The division now moved well away from Vitebsk even though strong Soviet forces continued to battle immediately to the southeast of the city, i.e., in the rear of the Germans. As early as 0700, advanced detachment Boineburg signalled that it was fighting in Kolyski 48 km almost due east to Vietbsk. Funck followed the advanced detachment with Pz.R.25 when at 1225 he received the order from corps headquarters to advance along an additional axis well to the north through Janovici. Funck, with some operational agility, ordered an element of the advance designated march group Lungerhausen and consisting of strong elements of S.R.7 to change direction and move through Janovici which lay 37 km northeast of Vitebsk. During the evening at 2020 the advanced elements of advanced detachment Boineburg reached Demidov 85 km from Vitebsk, and at 2330 on the other axis of advance Lungerhausen and S.R.7 seized Janovici.

Ominously though, strong Soviet forces continued to battle their way toward Vitebsk from the southeast.

Although Funck and the division staff never looked back over their shoulders, the rear elements of the division faced a crisis that threatened the advance of the entire XXXIX.Pz.K. north of Smolensk. At 0600 24 July 41, *Major i.G.* Liese, Ib, 7.Pz.D. coming back through Vietbsk from the advanced elements of the division ran into strong Soviet forces with infantry, tanks, and artillery only 3 km from the outskirts of Vitebsk on the great (wide but unpaved) main road from Smolensk. Liese ordered the drivers and assistant drivers of the trucks of the division supply columns with him to leave their vehicles and defend the road with rifles and machine guns. Looking around for assistance, Liese came on a German pioneer company and an infantry company nearby engaged in road repair and formed a blocking force now of several hundred men to halt the tough but cautious Soviets. By 0900, Liese, now in the Quartermaster Detachment (i.e., the logistics force of the division) command post, asked the Operations Staff of the division for assistance. The Ia of 7.Pz.D., now almost 100 km away to the east with the mass of the division, told Liese with a combination of coolness, concentration on the advance, and total underestimation of the dangers that there could be no help from division. Liese thereupon drove to the nearby command post of XXXIX. Pz.K., presented the advance-threatening crisis and observed the Chief of Staff of XXXIX. Pz.K order 1.R.90 (Mot.) of 20.1.D. (mot), i.e., an entire regiment from another division, to move immediately to save the situation.

The utter concentration of Funck and the operations staff on the advance is illustrated by the events of 14 July 41. The Ib had warned the Ia that the division supply line had been cut by the Soviet advance around 0600. Early in the afternoon, the division fuel and ammunition columns still could not move through the middle of the heavy battle that had developed as 1.R.90 (mot.) intervened in the fighting. The supply crises could not have been more real and immediate. Yet at

1534, the Ib received from the Ia a message that can be paraphrased as follows: where are your foremost supply columns? how is the march going? how much fuel has the supply detachment got with its columns? The Ib remarked in the Quartermaster war diary: "At the Quartermaster Detachment we received this message with absolute incomprehensibility."[58] At this juncture in the war in the east, Funck and the operations staff of 7.Pz.D. had some special sense of the great victory they were about to win and pressed on against a surprised and confused opponent. *Funck and the Ia showed steady nerves and a will to advance that matched the opportunity that presented itself.* Instead of turning about to address danger to the west, they continued to advance to take advantage of decisive operational opportunity to the east. At 2055 14 July 41, the advanced detachment of *Hauptmann* Schulz of Pz.R.25 stood at the lake narrows 20 km east southeast of Demidov and now 105 km *east* of powerful Soviet forces continuing to *attack* against 12.Pz.D. south of Vietbsk (See Map 6).

The next morning, 15 July 41, the division commander ordered the advance to begin to take the Minsk-Smolensk-Moscow "autobahn" near Ulchova-Sloboda approximately 48 km northeast of Smolensk. The Ib announced early in the morning that fuel columns had moved well beyond Vitebsk carrying 125 cbm (cubic meters: one cbm equivalent to 264 U.S. gallons) or 33,000 gallons of gasoline for the tanks of the division, all of which had gasoline engines, and the trucks, almost all of which had such engines. *Hauptmann* Schulz with the advanced detachment of the division passed through Duchovscina at 1730 and reached the Moscow-Smolensk "autobahn" at 1900 still during daylight. An hour and a half later, S.Brig.7 reached the "autobahn" in the immediate vicinity of Jarcewo. Troops and tanks of 7.Pz.D. stood blocking the unpaved, immense (in some places 100 feet wide) main line of road communication for approximately 500,000 Soviet troops

---

58.   See in, *7.Pz.D., Ib, Kriegstagebuch der Quartiermeister-Abteilung, 1. Juni 41-28. Januar 42, 14.7.41*, U.S., Archives, German Records, Divisions, T-315, Roll 423, Fr. 000045.

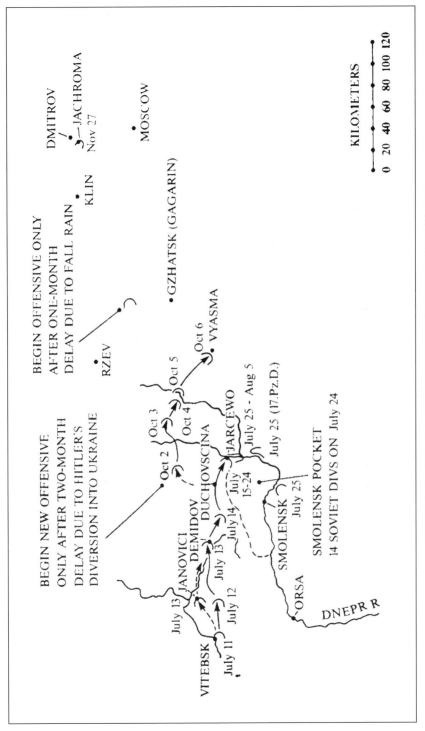

Map 6. Advance of 7.Pz.D. to Effect Encirclements at Smolensk and West of Vyasma.

lying far to the west and engaged with strong German forces which would now attempt to prevent their escape east.

In less than 48 hours on 14, 15 July 41, the division had moved more than 160 km through the Soviet Union, taken almost no casualties, and achieved a strategic-level, potentially war winning dislocation of the Soviet defenses in the forefield of Moscow now only about 190 km away. The division advanced with no friendly neighboring divisions keeping pace and with an extraordinarily challenging supply situation in terms of both the enemy and the unpaved and often extremely primitive Russian roads. On 15 July 41, Headquarters, VIII. Air Corps informed the division at 0915 that the main effort of the Luftwaffe for the day would be in support of its advance. The division moved with so great a tempo that it bowled over surprised Russian forces without need of ground attack sorties by the Luftwaffe. On the other hand, the war diary of the division records no Soviet air attack and the advancing Germans may have been given a special but not measurable impetus by the lighter aircraft of VIII. Air Corps in preventing air attack on the Germans' combat and supply columns. On the other hand, it is possible that 7.Pz.D. had been *lost* by the Soviet high command, which in turn would have been unable (obviously) to coordinate air or ground attack against a German division that was no longer on Soviet operational maps even remotely close to its actual location.

By the morning of 16 July 41, the Soviet high command knew exactly where 7.Pz.D. was located. Reconnaissance aircraft organic to 7.Pz.D. reported Soviet columns lined up one behind the other on the "autobahn" east of Jarcewo under German artillery fire.[59] By 0630, S.Brig.7 held a short stretch of "autobahn" effectively enough to prevent any further Soviet use for the rest of the battle. The division brought the rail station at Jarcewo under fire of heavy artillery (150mm

---

59.   See, for example, *7.Pz.D., Ia, Einsatz Ost, Band 1, Fleigermeldung, 16.7.41*, U.S., Archives, German Records, Divisions, T-315, Roll 410, Fr. 000752.

howitzers and long-barreled guns) at 0930. Just to the west of Jarcewo, S.Brig.7 signalled that it had blocked the rail line that ran parallel with the "autobahn" and was the main rail connection between Smolensk and Moscow. Located squarely on its target, 7.Pz.D. would stay fixed close to those positions blocking the main route of advance and withdrawal for the main concentration of the Red Army. 7.Pz.D. had demonstrated the technical mobility and firepower and the operational style to advance almost freely on several critical days through the Soviet Union. The question now was: had the division gone too far, too fast? Had it arrived with the combat capability, the critical operational mass necessary to defend itself and to hold what it had so daringly seized? Would it be successful when forced to remain virtually unmoved in fixed positions?

From 16 July-5 August 41, 7.Pz.D. defended itself against attacks from east and west with troop units sometimes placed almost back to back. See, for example, Maps 7 and 8 (in appendix) that show the situations on 25 and 28 July 41 in which 7.Pz.D. has finally linked up with 17.Pz.D., arriving from the south. Map 8 shows 7.Pz.D. on 28 July 41 in positions facing east and west and only 5 km apart, an intriguing situation for artillery and air support. For 7.Pz.D., the situation was a hair-raising one that called for strong nerves. Approximately 450,000 Soviet troops lay to the west of the division at this time and their direct line of escape looked down the Smolensk-Moscow "autobahn." To the east, the newly formed Soviet 24th Army stood with its route of advance lying down the same "autobahn" and slightly to the north of it. The great achievement of 7.Pz.D. had been to seize several kilometers of the "autobahn." The division stood there marked now for reinforcement by the Germans and extinction by the Soviets.

7.Pz.D. projected itself on 15 July 41 into a unique situation. The division had advanced so far that when it reached its target it found itself essentially in a void. It faced no coherent Soviet threat from the east or the west; there were many Soviet armed forces personnel around but they were concentrated in supply columns, columns of evacuated wounded, and loosely controlled reinforcements moving west. In effect, a German Panzer division lay "in the middle of" European Russia untouched by the Soviets for the two days of 16, 17 July 41 after its arrival. During the same period, the Soviets continued to awake to the dangers of the impending catastrophe in their Western Military District. On 15 July, the headquarters of the entire Soviet western front found itself in Smolensk now cut off from the rest of the Soviet Union along the main routes of movement. The Soviets reacted with their characteristic frenetic and casualty-producing energy, and during 18 and 19 July 41, launched extremely strong attacks from the east alongside of and right down the "autobahn." The attacks were uncoordinated with the huge force partly encircled to the west, and were also uncoordinated at the operational level among the divisions available for attack. Moreover, the attacks were uncoordinated at the tactical level with infantry, tanks, and artillery engaging independently of one another. The attacks failed on 18, 19 July and none would succeed in preventing the essential destruction of the Soviet forces to the west which would give up by approximately 3 August 41, 309,000 prisoners.

In the violent battles of 18 July 41, the Soviets attacked with about 100 tanks along the "autobahn" into the positions of a single German battalion, namely I./S.R.7, commanded by Major Weitzler. The battalion fought off the Soviet attack that began at 1635 with Flak, *Pak*, and artillery and claimed the destruction of 35 Soviet tanks. The Germans credited *Gefreiter Weiss*, a gunner on an 88mm Flak of I./Flak36, a Luftwaffe battalion attached at that moment to T.Pz.D., with the "shooting up" of 20 Soviet tanks alone.[60] Weiss, of course, fought as part of a gun crew, but he largely acquired the targets, laid the gun on them and made all of the subtle adjustments necessary to get the

---

60. See in, *7.Pz.D., Ia, Einsatz, Ost, Band 1, Berichte, 19.7.1941*, U.S., National Archives, German Records, Divisions, T-315, Roll 410, Fr. 000738.

rounds on target in direct fire. The incident shows the Germans at their tactical best. In it, a private in the Luftwaffe has the skill in firing an antiaircraft gun that had been thoughtfully provided with ground firing optics during its prewar development to achieve an operational level result in the single most important engagement fought that day on the eastern front. This achievement was not lost on the German command. At 2200 that evening, the commander of II./Flak 38 arrived at the division command post and announced that his 8. and 9. batteries were on the way to reinforce the defense.

During the fighting noted above, the division ordered Pz.R.25 into the area northwest of Fomina near Duchovscina against a strong enemy advancing from the *west* into the division defensive perimeter. This fighting developed during the early evening of 18 July 41 and involved numbers of tanks on both sides. The Germans employed Flak, *Pak*, and artillery in support of their tanks as the fighting continued on into the hours of darkness. Pz.R.25 counted 25 Soviet tanks lying immobilized or destroyed in front of its position the next morning. In fighting this successful action, Pz.R.25 (with IL/A.R.78 attached) secured the division main supply route from Duchovscina to Jarcewo and began to set the lines of encirclement around the Soviet forces at Smolensk. The situation had been chaotic and dangerous along that route; for example, earlier at 0230 on 18 July 41, the road had been overrun by the Soviets farther west about halfway to Demidov. The Soviets there had attacked also from the west but the successful action of Pz.R.25 and units of 20.Pz.D. on the same day began to stabilize the German lines of encirclement.

Early the next morning, 19 July 41, as directed by corps, I./ S.R.112 arrived from 20.Pz.D. to support the German defense of the "autobahn." Later at 0905, Headquarters, VIII. Air Corps informed 7.Pz.D. that it would be supported by the considerable total of 56 combat aircraft during the day. After getting increasing evidence of the Soviets massing for an attack, the division abruptly came under attack by approximately 80 Soviet tanks again in the vicinity of the "autobahn" near Jarcewo. The Soviets attacked with tanks and infantry well supported by artillery and "bombers" even though the Soviet Air Force suffered from catastrophic losses in aircraft - the Germans had destroyed on the ground or in the air approximately 2,050 Soviet aircraft in the first 17 *hours* of the war alone. The German motorized infantry comprising approximately two battalions at this time supported by a Panzer company successfully held the positions all along the line. As the division swung to the defensive, the Ia directed that the first priority in resupply be changed from fuel to ammunition - specifically artillery ammunition.

At midnight on 19 July 41, Funck and his division still faced an acute situation in survival. The main supply route continued to be difficult to move along and the division was not yet linked with neighbors on either side. In the middle of the night Funck and the Ia worked to get as strong Stuka dive bomber support as possible for the next day. Various battalion and regimental level organizations of the division changed the locations of their command posts during the early morning from 0000-0400 and S.Brig.7 suffered from having all of its internal telephone lines cut by the intense Soviet artillery fire. Between 0745 and 1100, Stuka (Ju 87) dive bombers and He III two-engined tactical bombers make attacks that reduced the Soviet artillery fire to a more acceptable level. By noon on 20 July 41, corps headquarters had begun to coordinate the movement of 12.Pz.D. into position on the division left and 20.I.D. (mot.) on the right. Units of those two divisions began to arrive alongside of 7.Pz.D. by the evening and stabilize the situation.

During the period 21-23 July, the three divisions organized their defenses to prevent the breaking or breakout of Soviet forces on the central front along the Moscow "autobahn." At the same time, the Soviet high command continued the formation of the new 24th Army specifically ordering a powerful element of several divisions designated as Group Kalinin to breakthrough the German positions on an axis running through Duchovscine, i.e., a line running through 12.Pz.D. and into the rear of 7.Pz.D. and 20.1.D. (mot.), to destroy those German forces and maintain the front around Smolensk. Map 9 (in appendix) illustrates how 12.Pz.D. counterattacked to destroy Group Kalinin and 7.Pz.D. maintained its positions around Jarcewo on 24 July 41. On 25 July 41, 7.Pz.D. edged several kilometers south of the "autobahn" to link up with 17.Pz.D. and for the next several days from 26 July-August 41 fought successfully to effect the destruction of the Soviet forces now trapped around Smolensk. Later, on the evening of 5-6 August 41, 7.Pz.D. was relieved by an infantry division and went into rest positions behind the lines northeast of Smolensk. Soon thereafter the war would change for Germany, and although 7.Pz.D. fought often and well, never again would they have the opportunity to achieve strategically what they had in the past.

Chapter 3

Observations on the Combat Performance of the 7th Panzer Division and Suggested Actions for the Improvement of Marine Corps Operational Capabilities

Under a renowned commander of World War II (Rommel), 7.Pz.D. achieved extraordinary results fighting on the offensive in France in 1940. Under a commander unknown today (Funck), the division achieved even more extraordinary results in the opening stages of the surprise offensive against the Soviet Union in 1941. In both cases the division engaged first class opponents who had vast resources in men and materiel. In both cases, the Germans advanced against opponents well prepared for war, but utterly surprised by the division's direction, timing, violence and above all, tempo. The word "tempo" describes the Germans and particularly 7.Pz.D. on the offensive, or more precisely, the phrase: "tempo prestissimo" rapid tempo.

The Germans were so successful at the tactical and operational levels in part due to their historic circumstances. From the 1890s and thereafter, they faced powerful coalitions whose strengths lay in resources, blockades, and attrition. The Germans, if they were to succeed, had to conduct brief, overpowering ground offensives against numerous enemies conducting unhurried siege operations against them. As "prisoners" of their historical condition, the Germans had to fight battles and conduct operations more effectively than any of their enemies. Having to conduct ground combat more effectively than any other nation, the Germans, in fact, in two world wars did exactly that.

While they were ultimately defeated at the strategic level, their tactical and operational achievements remain unmatched. The question for all other western ground forces today is whether the superior warfighting style of the Germans is transferable.

The uniqueness of the German historic situation is accentuated when we look farther back in time to the 1700s and early 1800s. The army and general staff of Prussia gave its command style and combat spirit to the German army of 1914-1945. Prussia stood surrounded during that earlier period by strong natural enemies and survived only by some special insights into war fighting not quite achieved by any other armed force to the present day. Prussia transferred the tradition of a great captain (Frederick I), the flexibility of the reformers of the Napoleonic period (Scharnhorst), the insights of a philosopher of war (Clausewitz), and succinct, practical style of a great chief of staff (Moltke) to a later army of 1914-1945 that continued to have to attack to win. It can be no surprise, therefore, that the German army operated on the offensive more effectively than any other.

But how can U.S. ground forces today conduct offensive operations better than at present within the framework of a military tradition of war since 1914 as an exercise in logistics, and a present day political stance that concedes to the opponent the great opening offensive in which the Germans sparkled? Under such circumstances, is it even possible to transfer the superior German style in offensive operation to U.S. ground forces "imprisoned" by so different a set of historical circumstances? The answer to these questions is yes we can learn from the Germans, but it is harder than it seems. For example, the Germans, using the Prussian General Staff, defeated France decisively in 1870-71. This caused every important power of the world (including the United States with its small army of the day) to develop a general staff system based on the Prussian-German model. Not one state, however, was able to do more than follow the form while essentially failing to understand the content.

What then was the "content" of the advance of the 7.Pz.D in France in 1940 and the Soviet Union in 1941? The Germans of 1940 and 1941 accepted the uncertainty in war. The U.S. Army and the Marine Corps, at times seem to almost fear uncertainty. They attempt to eradicate uncertainty in war and as a result demand that officers and noncommissioned officers not make mistakes. The German army embraced the central reality of uncertainty in war and rode it to operations of unparelleled tempo and daring. The German army encouraged its men to act and accepted the fact that they would make mistakes. 7.Pz.D. exemplified this philosophy: it was always right to act; it was always wrong to wait for more information, more troops, more fire support to clear up uncertainty. Rommel and Funck and the division exemplified this willingness to accept uncertainty, this determination to act, this preference of the oral order over the written. Commanders must command. The staff are expediters, few in numbers, modest in rank but long in self confidence and initiative.

It may be difficult for other western armies to achieve the tempo regularly maintained by 7.Pz.D.. The Germans, which 7.Pz.D. represents so well, had a unique historical development and bolder approach to the realities of combat. It may be possible to test or practice, nevertheless, some of the techniques and the style of the Germans that specifically defined tempo in 7.Pz.D.. If in test and practice, the specific techniques and style prove to be transferable, it can be assumed that the western ground force modified thusly would be a far more dangerous animal on the offensive. A *First Observation* that can be made on the dramatic drive of 7.Pz.D. under Rommel from the Belgian border to Arras in Northwestern France is that *the division advanced and fought 24 hours a day.*

7.Pz.D. fought in a pattern in which it consistently reached its targets for "the day" (24-hour day) early in the evening, reorganized, and advanced toward the next day's target at approximately the middle of the night, 7.Pz.D. and other German divisions, did roughly as much fighting and moving at night as they did during the long summer hours of daylight. Virtually all of the photographs taken in the campaign and the written descriptions result in an extremely misleading picture of the campaign. The photographs, of technical necessity, are almost exclusively daylight scenes. Works on the campaign dwell similarly on the "days," i.e., "implied" daylight hours, of the campaign. There is an important exception in the night evacuation of British and French troops by *sea*, but even these scenes tend to reinforce the picture of war in a summer sun during almost all of the campaign. The Germans of 7.Pz.D. operated 24 hours a day and slept whenever they could; all this apparently, without any "doctrine" on the matter. Unlike the Israelis who self consciously tout their "concept" of fighting 24 hours a day in a mini, ultra-brief advance as in the June 1967 war, the Germans seemed almost "instinctively" to have fought 24 hours a day.

But, of course, the success of the 7.Pz.D was more than just 24 hour operations. The German commanders of tank divisions stationed themselves forward in the mobile advance. The Ia of the German division dominated the extremely small division staff that in turn had little inertia or friction in its parts. No "Chief" had to be consulted by a commanding officer in a German division to get on the division commander's calendar. There was no chief; there was an officer skilled in advising the commander on the operations of the division in war and keeping track of the fighting. This officer had neither the rank nor the inclination to get between the commanding general and his subordinate commanders. His humility ended there, however, because he issued orders in the name of the commander binding on the entire division. This officer also functioned unquestioned even when it was apparent that he was acting independently in crises that demanded action.

The division was never slowed by friction, over-planning, and debate in the staff. The Commander's will dominated the scene, not the bureaucratic, decisionless presence of the staff. If the division commander had even the casual inclination to advance, he and the division advanced. With so little inertia and friction in the command style and organization of the division, when the division commander moved, the division moved with him.

The Germans manned and organized the staffs of their divisions in a way that encouraged their decisiveness and speed in combat. Every German division in 1939 and thereafter in World War II referred to the officers in the enumerated positions Ia, Ib, and Ic in various ways including operations officer, quartermaster, and intelligence officer respectively and also first general staff officer for operations, first general staff officer for supply, and first general staff officer for intelligence. Only the Ia and Ib, however, were ever actual general staff officers, i.e., officers who had been selected to go to the two-year course at the *Kriegsakademie* (War Academy) and had successfully completed that education.[61] (Any statement that the German division had three general staff officers is therefore misleading.[62])

In the division, there was an Operations Staff (*Fuhrungs Staffel*) that included the Ia, Ib and IIa (Personnel) and concentrated on operational matters. There was also a Quartermaster Staff (*Quartiermeister Staffel*) in the division that included the Ib and several staff assistants. General Staff Officers were a rare commodity. They had fabled competence, and the division commander depended on them to provide the necessary staff work and staff supervision. The two officers did just that. The Ia supervised operations, the Ib supervised supply and everything else. They did so through the two staffs noted above and the Operations and Quartermaster Detachments respectively controlled by them.

---

61. See, for example, *Das Deutsche Heer 1939, Gliederung, Stellenbesetezung, Verzeichnis samtlicher Offiziere am 3.1.1939*, Herausgegeben von H.H. Podzun (Bad Nauheim, 1953), in which all 51 of the full strength German peacetime divisions of early 1939 are shown as having two general staff officers.

62. See, Martin van Creveld, *Fighting Power, German Military Performance, 1914-1945* (Washington, D.C., December 1980), pp. 55, 56. The diagram here just combines the "three general staff officers" in a "Section I, Operations" and is misleading also because there was no *Staffel* and no detachment in a German division that included the Ia, Ib, and Ic.

To illustrate the streamlined style of the Germans in staff functioning, compare the staff of 7.Pz.D. with Marine Corps staffs. Figure 24 contrasts the "staff" of the 7.Pz.D., a formation of approximately 15,500 personnel and 284 tanks in June 41, with the staff of a Marine Corps infantry *battalion* of 1989. The immediate general staff sections of the German Panzer *division* contained seven staff officers (3 Majors, 4 Captains) in contrast to the parallel immediate battalion staff sections of the Marine Corps infantry *battalion* with 12 staff officers (2 Majors, 5 Captains, 5 Lieutenants). The staff officers in the immediate staff sections of a Marine infantry *battalion* (1989) outnumber the parallel German staff officers of a German Panzer *division* (1941) by a factor of almost two to one. The contrast is so extreme that it cannot be explained in terms of the special necessities of amphibious operations and the increasing technical (hardware) complexity of war.

It would be reasonable also to contrast the staff of 7.Pz.D. with that of the present day Marine Corps division. Figure 25 contrasts the same "staff" of 7.Pz.D. discussed above with the staff of a Marine division as authorized by T/O 1986G of 10 January 1989 and found in the "Div HQ HQ CO HQ BN MAR DIV." The figure shows the same seven staff officers of 7.Pz.D. lined up against the parallel staff officers of the staff sections of the headquarters of the Marine division. Including the Assistant Division Commander, the division included 30 officers distributed as follows: 1 BGen, 6 Col, 11 LtCol, 11 Maj, and 7 Capt. In the case of this comparison, the Marine staff officers outnumber the Germans by more than four to one. The story does not end here, however, because the comparison should also take account in some way of the higher ranks of the Marine officers. Assigning the present day numbers for officer ranks of 1 through 9 (i.e., derived from 01-09) to get an idea of the weight in terms of the ranks of the two staffs, we get a rank weight of 24 for 7.Pz.D. and a contrasting weight of 163 for the modern Marine division with the Marine staff outweighing the Germans by a factor of almost seven to one.

Why fundamentally has the Marine Corps come to put together a small city around its division commander? The key to this is probably the previously discussed factor of uncertainty in war. With its armed violence and accompanying chaos, war *is* the realm of uncertainty and chance. The immense staff of a Marine division can be seen as an attempt to remove uncertainly from combat. The greater the numbers

---

Marine Infantry Battalion (1989)
(LtCol) Battalion Commander
(Maj) Battalion XO

S-1	S-2	S-3	S-4
(Capt) S-1/Adj	(Capt) S-2 Intel	(Maj) S-3	(Capt) S-4
(Lt) Pers		(Capt) Asst S-3	(Lt) S-4A Embark
		(Lt) Liaison	(Lt) S-4A MMO
		(Capt) Asst S-3	
		(Lt) Asst S-3 FAC	

Totals
12 Officers:
  2 Maj
  5 Capt
  5 Lt

plus several special staff officers in support of entire battalion

---

German 7th Panzer Division (1941)
(BGen) Division Commander

Operations Staff	Quartermaster Staff
(Maj) Ia OPS	(Maj) Ib Quartermaster
(Capt) Asst Ia	(Capt) Asst Ib
(Capt) Ic Intel	
(Maj) IIa Pers	
(Capt) Asst IIa	

Totals
7 Officers:
  3 Maj
  4 Capt

plus modest number of special staff officers in the Quartermaster Detachment

Figure 24. Contrasting Marine Infantry Battalion and German 7th Panzer Division Staff Sections.

Marine Infantry Battalion (1989)
(MGen) Division Commander
(BGen) Asst Div Commander
(Col) Chief of Staff W/(Maj) Ops
Analysis (Capt) Asst

G-1	G-2	G-3	G-4
(Col) G-1	(Col) G-2	(Col) G-3	(Col) G-4
(LtCol) Asst G-1	(LtCol) Asst G-2	(LtCol) Asst G-3	(LtCol) Asst G-4
(Maj) Asst G-1	(LtCol) Asst	(LtCol) OPS	(LtCol) Plans
(LtCol) Human	(LtCol) Intell	(Maj) Asst OPS	(Maj) Plans
(Maj) Drugs	(Capt) Analysis	(Maj) Civ Affairs	(Maj) OPS
(Capt) Affirm		(Capt) Asst EW	(Capt) Asst OPS
		(LtCol) WPNS	
		Employ	
		plus	plus
		innumerable	(Col) Asst C/S
		special staff	Readiness
		officers in H&S Bn	

Totals
30 Officers:

1 BGen	11 Maj
6 Col	7 Capt
11 LtCol	

German 7th Panzer Division (1941)
(BGen) Division Commander

Operations Staff

(Maj) Ia
(Capt) Asst Ia
(Capt) Ic Intel
(Maj) IIa Pers
(Capt) Asst IIa

Quartermaster Staff

(Maj) Ib Quartermaster
(Capt) Asst Ib

plus
modest number of special staff
officers in the Quartermaster
Detachment

Totals
7 Officers:
  3 Maj
  4 Capt

Figure 25. Contrasting Marine Division and German 7th Panzer Division Staff Sections.

of officers, the higher their ranks, the more information they can gather, all of these things represent a fundamental urge to remove uncertainty from war. In their divisions, the Germans confronted uncertainty with action. The Ia dominated the small staff and ensured that priority went to operational action. The size of the Marine staff, in contrast, shows that it tends to concentrate on removing uncertainty and guaranteeing success through plan and preparation rather than mobile action. Unless this fundamental error is confronted and changed, it will be difficult to reduce the size of staffs and make rapid tempo a constant.

Which brings us to the first of six suggested actions:

7.Pz.D. Project Suggested Action #1

Based on the striking differences in size and rank between the staffs of the Marine division (1989) and the German 7th Panzer Division (1941), the Marine Corps should form an experimental staff unit. Such an experiment would emphasize simulated combat on the offensive and would use the organization and style of the 7th Panzer Division as a guide to the possibilities of improved operational capability.

Associated with rapid tempo, Rommel introduced into 7.Pz.D. the use of the *Stosslinie* (thrust line) to direct movements of the division, to locate any unit or person, and to direct supporting fire. Depending upon the situation, division headquarters would pass the thrust line as part of a written operations order or by radio message. Thrust lines would begin and end at clearly defined points on the appropriate operational maps and would be in effect for a day or more. The thrust line had a brilliant psychological component to it because it pointed every unit and man in the division along a clear main axis. Perhaps more than anything, the thrust line was graphic. It pointed the way unmistakably. On 15 July 41, Funck drew the thrust line boldly to the train station at Jarcewo astride the mail rail line between Smolensk and

Moscow. The successful use of the thrust line suggests the following action on the part of the Marine Corps today:

7.Pz.D. Project Suggested Action #2

Based on the conceptualization of a great commander of World War II and the successful application of the concept by him and others in 7.Pz.D. in 1940 and 1941, the Marine Corps should experiment through map exercises and organizational tests with use of thrust lines for Marine Corps operations in offensive situations.

Clearly any review of the 7.Pz.D. and its rapid tempo suggests that the Marine Corps might profitably test its offensive capabilities by using combat scenarios that demand distant, rapid movement on the part of the division. The Marine Corps should test using both field exercises and map exercise problems (particularly at places like the Command and Staff College). The question should be, does the Marine Corps have the style and capabilities to perform as effectively as a division like the 7.Pz.D.? Scenarios should be chosen so that the entire division is tested in its capabilities to move out from a beachhead in deep mobile offensive operations. There is no intention in any of this to convert a Marine division into a "tank heavy," armored division; the idea is simply to study and test its capabilities to move quickly as a motorized division with, of course, special modern assets such as transport helicopters.

The Marine Corps should also consider adding additional mobility to units within its divisions. In 7.Pz.D. one Panzer regiment and two motorized infantry regiments were its most important maneuver units. Unlike a Marine division today, which has an amphibious reconnaissance battalion but no real ground reconnaissance battalion, 7.Pz.D. had an armored reconnaissance detachment *and* a motorcycle battalion. The motorcycle battalion tended to get lost in the organization diagrams of the day by being placed within the motorized rifle brigade of 7.Pz.D.. The motorcycle battalion (K.7) of the division, however, was used almost exclusively by the division commander, who employed it reinforced as the advanced detachment of the division or as a characteristic, German-style, *Kampfgruppe*, maneuver element. The division commander employed the armored reconnaissance detachment (Pz.A.A.37) almost identically. The end result: the 7.Pz.D. and every other German armored division of the day had essentially *two* reconnaissance or "advanced detachment" style battalions.

Under the fluid conditions of a major offensive, the division commander had the capability to keep things moving along two axes of advance. In France, Rommel would often send off K.7 in advance of the rest of the division and on several occasions personally accompanied it in a couple of armored reconnaissance vehicles. Under such conditions, Rommel often orchestrated a second axis of advance somewhat to the rear and led by Pz.A.A.37 in a stronger *Kampfgruppe* in which it was the advanced detachment. In the Soviet Union, Funck used K.7 and Pz.A.A.37 similarly, and in the dramatic rush to the Moscow Autobahn near Jarcewo on 14, 15, July 41, he had these particularly mobile elements moving along two axes of advance. K.7, with its two motorcycle companies and weapons company of 80mm mortars and *Pak* guns struck an effective balance between low "starting inertia" and combat power. Pz.AA.37, with its two armored reconnaissance vehicle companies, motorcycle company and mobile supporting infantry cannon, struck the same kind of balance.

If the Marine Corps is interested in being able to mount a rapid mobile advance out of a beachhead, it should experiment with the formation of either an armored reconnaissance battalion or a battalion with special mobility analogous to that of the motorcycle battalion in the German Panzer division. The success of 7.Pz.D. in deep mobile advances serves as evidence for the inclusion of both a reconnaissance *and* an additional mobile battalion in a Marine division. We should not reduce the capability of the Marine division to seize a different beachhead in the first place or defend it in the event of very strong opposition. The division, however, while retaining the capability to make an opposed landing, should have the additional capability and command style to advance out of a beachhead to seize distant targets on its own. In many modern scenarios, the division may be called on to exploit its *strategic mobility* to make an *unopposed* landing in which case its *operational mobility* ashore becomes relatively more important. In such a case, the premium would be on the mobility to advance deeply and boldly. For text, it would require units similar to those which 7.Pz.D. found indispensible in its advances of 1940 and 1941. Which leads to the following suggested action:

7.Pz.D. Project Suggested Action #3

Based on the extraordinary effectiveness of the German 7.Pz.D. on the offensive in World War II, the Marine Corps should put together an experimental armored reconnaissance battalion for inclusion in the Marine division and test the formation in scenarios that center on rapid, distant advance beyond beachheads in both opposed and unopposed landings. In order to increase the capability of the Marine division to advance rapidly on two axes, the Marine Corps should calculate the desirability of an additional mobile formation of battalion level in the division analogous to the German motorcycle battalion.

The "reconnaissance" battalion would have the capability to conduct ground reconnaissance both in depth and breadth and to screen the movement of the division on the offense and defense. The "motorcycle" battalion would have special capabilities in ground reconnaissance and screening and, additionally, could be armed and manned to provide significant strength in offensive and defensive combat. The division commander would have ready-made in both battalions "advanced detachments" to lead the division in a deep advance of the entire division.

The commanders of 7.Pz.D. employed heavy weapons in a style that holds lessons for the Marine Corps today. Under both Rommel and Funck, 7.Pz.D. employed 20mm and 88mm Flak cannon against enemy infantry and tanks. The heavy Flak employed by the division scored impressive successes against the French and Soviet heavy tanks (Char B, SOMUA and KV-1, 2, T-34); and, the light automatic Flak proved effective against Soviet infantry and the lightly armored T-26 infantry support and BT-5, 7 fast tanks. The Germans faced a cruel dilemma in such employment because the greater the success of Flak against tanks and infantry, the more it would be used against them and the less it would be available to carry out the primary mission of shooting down enemy aircraft. The Commanding General, XXXDCPz.K. in a directive of July 41 summed up the German situation by first admonishing Funck and his other division commanders for excessive casualties among Flak crews that had been pushed to the ground front in various crises; he warned them to save the Flak for air defense. He concluded the directive, however, by stating that tank attack more than any other factor could result in the *destruction* of the division and that every Flak available would be pressed into use for the defense of the division when necessary.[63]

Working systematically in the 1930s, the Germans had developed the 88mm Flak 36 technically into a dual purpose cannon. In a less well known case, they had employed the cannon in the Polish Campaign in an experimental heavy antitank battalion to test the tactical potential of the weapon in ground combat. By the time of the French Campaign, they were ready to use the weapon against aircraft, tanks, and against modern steel reinforced concrete fortifications. No other power in World War II employed its antiaircraft weapons so flexibly. 7.Pz.D. exemplified the employment in successes achieved against Allied tanks in the west in 1940 and even greater successes against Soviet tanks

---

63. See in, *7.Pz.D., Ia, Einsatz Ost, Band 2, Generalkommando XXXIXA.K., Abteilung Ia, K. Gef. St., den 25.7.1941, Betr.: Einsatz der Flakartillerie*, U.S., Archives, German Records Division. T-315, Roll 410, Fr. 000707.

and infantry in the east in 1941. The Germans proved capable through some combination of systematic technical development *and* tactical spontaneity in extracting the most out of their weapons. *Gefreiter* Weiss highlighted all of this when he put out of action 20 Soviet tanks on 18 July 41, a single individual achieving an operational level result using an antiaircraft gun against tough opponents like the Soviets. The Marines can learn from such actions.

7.Pz.D. Project Suggested Action #4
Based on the German employment of the 88mm antiaircraft gun in ground combat as high-lighted by the 7.Pz.D. in France and the Soviet Union, the Marine Corps should reexamine every ongoing development of antiaircraft weapons to ensure the development of dual purpose weapons capable of firing at ground targets.

Based on the same premises, the Marine Corps should test the capabilities of existing antiaircraft weapons available to it, e.g., weapons like Stinger and Redeye, against ground targets. Similarly, but with the direction of approach reversed, the Marine Corps should test the capabilities of its ground weapons such as tank cannon, light automatic cannon, and artillery against air targets.

7.Pz.D. creatively used other weapons and equipment with verifiably effective results. The division received no close air support in the style of the Marine Corps. The division received strong air support from the Stuka dive bombers directed characteristically against artillery positions, tank assembly areas, and columns of tanks and vehicles on the road. The German air attacks in support of 7.Pz.D. took place almost universally at least a kilometer or more away from the positions of the division. Interrogations of prisoners conducted by the Ic staff in the Operations Detachment of the division show that the German air attacks disrupted Allied road movements and silenced artillery, the latter effect often taking place due to the presence of the Stukas. In the East, German air attacks broke up potential Soviet tank attacks by disorganizing strong armored formations in their assembly areas and reduced artillery fire to acceptable levels or silenced it. The redoubtable *Oberst* Hans-Ulrich Rudel with strong claim to being the outstanding combat pilot in the history of military aviation received his *E.K.I*, on 18 July 41 largely for successful Stuka attacks against Soviet artillery positions.[64] In France, Rommel personally called for air attacks by Stukas several kilometers in front of his columns to "scatter" enemy forces. In the Soviet Union, Soviet prisoners consistently reported having experienced attack against their units on the move, with the result that their units became disorganized and "scattered."[65] The pattern of German air attack was clear and the results effective. In considering the requirements of mobile warfare, the Marine Corps would be advised at least to compare and contrast the effectiveness of close air support as presently conducted with an eye toward trading it for "pretty close air support" as conducted by the Germans in their offensives in 1940 and 1941.

7.Pz.D. used light signals as a common means of communicating important, time sensitive information. In contrast to the U.S. preference for smoke grenades, the Germans emphasized several varieties of rounds fired from a 27mm flare pistol. For the first day of the war against the Soviet Union, the division designated white star clusters especially as fired from the flare pistol as the signal to mark the front lines of the 7.Pz.D. in the ultra fluid conditions of the first hours of combat. Visible from long distance from the air and on the ground, light signals are an instantaneously effective way of alerting general and private soldier alike to momentary certainty in a sea of doubt. In support of 7.Pz.D., the Luftwaffe used red parachute flares dropped over Soviet tank assembly areas discovered near Jarcewo in close proximity (several kilometers) to division units and unknown at that

---

64. *Interview.* Hans-Ulrich Rudel, Kufstein, Austria, October 1978.
65. The Germans characteristically used the word *versprengte* (scattered) to describe the condition of enemy troops hit hard by their attack. The word appears repeatedly in the records.

moment to the ground troops. The Luftwaffe used the same signal later in July 41 to alert 7.Pz.D. troops immediately to the danger of Soviet tanks already advancing toward the German lines. Within seconds of the signals being released hundreds of Germans knew immediately what was coming and from where. During the same time period, 7.Pz.D. employed green star clusters fired from the ground towards the enemy to indicate the German front line for the Luftwaffe. The German experience suggests the following action:

7.Pz.D. Project Suggested Action #5

Based on the successful use of projected light signals from flare guns by 7.Pz.D. (and most other German combat formations), the Marine Corps should examine the advantages and disadvantages of projected signals and test available military and life saving flare pistols including projectors based on the M79 Grenade Launcher.

The Germans developed a 16-man pneumatic rubber raft and a nine-man wooden assault boat for pioneer units for support of river crossings. 7.Pz.D. found the large boat *(grosser Flossack)* with its 5,500-lb capacity extremely useful in the numerous river and canal crossings that punctuated the French Campaign and recommended in its report of experiences in the battle that the boat be issued to the motorized rifle regiments and the motorcycle battalion. The Germans designed the assault boat to sit low in the water and equipped it with an extremely well designed outboard motor. The big pneumatic boat although oared by a crew of seven, could be equipped with a motor and proved to be extremely successful as a ferry with several lashed together to carry trucks, guns, and supplies. Oars may sound a bit primitive today, but at several junctures in World War II, engines on assault boats could not be used because of the absolute tactical necessity to achieve surprise, for example, at night and in fog. The Marine Corps remains in an unusual condition in terms of river crossings; the Marine division has amphibious vehicles for ship to shore movement and a surfeit of transport helicopters. The very different tactical circumstance of mobile offensive combat ashore suggests that a study of the problems presented by inland water barriers would turn up real challenges. The German experience suggests that a relatively light pneumatic style boat/ferry might be a useful item for the Marine Corps.

In his report on experiences of the French Campaign, the division commander essentially demanded that 7.Pz.D. be reequipped with two "K" type bridging columns for Pi.58, the division pioneer battalion. In the campaign, Pi.58 held only one older "B" style bridging column and was not able to react effectively enough for Rommel in the rapid pace of the division across the numerous Belgian and French rivers and canals. Somewhat surprisingly, the Germans with their well-known technical thoroughness had failed to incorporate two bridge columns in the pioneer company so that *two* water courses could be crossed by the fast moving Panzer division which sometimes found itself facing a second water course while the division bridging had not yet been retrieved from the previous crossing. The Marine Corps could find it productive to look into a new balance in bridging columns and equipment and light river crossing pneumatic style boats for a Marine division reorienting itself in the direction of mobile warfare.

From the viewpoint of command and control, 7.Pz.D. had an item of equipment that proved itself throughout the war and had been developed in the interwar period. The division held *Panzer I*, and *Panzer 38(t)* tanks that had been modified and converted into command vehicles for commanders of elements of Pz.R.25. These tanks qua (in the capacity of) command vehicles possessed the mobility and armor protection of tanks. German commanders in these special tanks had the capability to move anywhere in the battle with vehicles having the armor and mobility of the strongest weapon in the division and without attracting special attention. In the case of the *Panzer III* version of the command tank, the Germans removed the main gun, replaced it with a *wooden* dummy barrel, and produced a vehicle with adequate space for map tables and additional radio equipment. It would be reasonable for the Marine division to leave two such vehicles for the use of the tank battalion CO and XO with the latter vehicle "available" for use of the division commander.

In the area of supply, 7.Pz.D. faced illuminating problems in keeping the fuel and ammunition columns of the division up with the mobile combat elements. Records of 7.Pz.D. reveal a two-fold problem. In big offensives involving strong friendly forces, the supply columns had difficulties getting through friendly traffic behind the advancing combat troops. Also, the division sometimes faced disastrous attacks on supply columns from surviving enemy forces along the route of advance. In the Soviet Union, the Ib pleaded for the setting up of a convoy system for the columns which was eventually established for a short period in the last days of June 41 northeast of Minsk. In the war diary of the Ib, the quartermaster discussed the situation and recorded the suggestion that the supply columns include combat escort units of light armored vehicles as part of their tables of organization and equipment for the future.

As a final tactical note, it should be pointed out that the commanders and staff of 7.Pz.D. characteristically put together battle groups *(Kampfgruppen)* sometimes several each day to accomplish tasks assigned on the mobile offense. The process of advance in 7.Pz.D. can be seen almost as the formation of one battle group after another. The division staff put these groups together almost entirely on the basis of oral orders and brief messages - written division operations orders were a rarity. In accordance with the will of the division commander, the Ia and the modest staff section around him spent most of their time putting together battle groups, assigning mission oriented tasks to them, keeping track of their movements and then rejuggling as the situation rapidly changed. On the offensive, the division staff existed to act and facilitate the action necessary to take advantage of opportunities.

Rommel in a message to division simply says "pioneers to the front." The Ia did not write an operations order to make this happen. The Ia clarified in his own mind how much and where and would probably have sent a message to Pi.58: "1 company immediately 25 right 1 km supporting crossing, attach 1 platoon *Pak*." Here we see things happening. The Ia alerts a commander, forms a small battle group, and gets things moving toward the front. The innumerable German battle groups and task groups suggest the following:

7.Pz.D. Project Suggested Action #6

Based on the observed success of 7.Pz.D. using one newly formed battle group after another, the Marine Corps should develop scenarios that demand rapid forward movement and which test the ability of commanders and staffs to put together battle groups both on the map and in field exercises.

In France, 7.Pz.D. advanced so effectively under Rommel that the conclusion for the Marine Corps could well be simply to fight on the offensive as Rommel and 7.Pz.D. did in 1940. Clausewitz should have liked this advice because while he appreciated that there are no rules in war, he recognized the decisive role of genius. To fight as Rommel did is to do as the genius does. The genius and his division advanced at a high tempo, fought 24 hours a day, would suffer no tactical impasse, applied every weapon of the division to the fight and created stratagem after stratagem to keep things moving. The Marine division on the offensive should do all of these things. But it is not so easy to do, as to suggest. The unique history and circumstances of the Germans made it necessary for them to excel in war. They grasped the essence of war: chaos, violence, uncertainty, chance, and danger. They determined in a long process of more than two centuries to meet uncertainly with action. Rommel's genius was action. This genius for action was built in to the structure of 7.Pz.D. through the small action oriented staff and the similarly oriented subordinate commanders.

In Russia, 7.Pz.D. advanced without Rommel even more effectively than it had in 1940. The Russian experience tells us that the genius of the division went far beyond one man. The great advances of 7.Pz.D. in Russia were based on self confidence and initiative among commanders, staff and rank and file - qualities that focus on rapid action in war. The senior commanders in 7.Pz.D. allowed subordinate leaders to make mistakes. The tolerance of these leaders was never an excuse for slipshod performance; it was the calm recognition that rapid action in the face of uncertainty will result in errors - errors that can be overcome by more action. German command style pivoted on taking action in war, demanded that subordinate leaders take such action, and accepted the mistakes that naturally occurred. With such a style, the leaders of 7.Pz.D. understood uncertainty as an omnipresent reality and rode with it to victories that cry out for emulation.

The Marine Corps is far different from the German army of 1940-1941 in historical condition and strategic mission. The premise of this study has been that the Marine Corps can learn much from the experience of the Germans on the mobile offensive, a role in which a Marine division could easily be cast in the future as a part of a Marine Expeditionary Force. The main conclusion of this work is that the Marine Corps can increase its operational capabilities by examining, testing, and putting in practice aspects of the organization, tactics, and style of a German Panzer division. The Marine Corps should take a particularly close look at the formation of battle groups, the concept of fighting 24 hours a day, and the concept of uncertainty in war. These are just the main lessons the 7.Pz.D. has to offer. There are others. The lessons lay in the pages of history like free money waiting for a Marine who is willing to snatch them up, take them back to his unit, and put them into action. The 7.Pz.D. did have a bias for action. On the next battlefield, any military force able to develop and practice that same bias will prove formidable.

Appendix

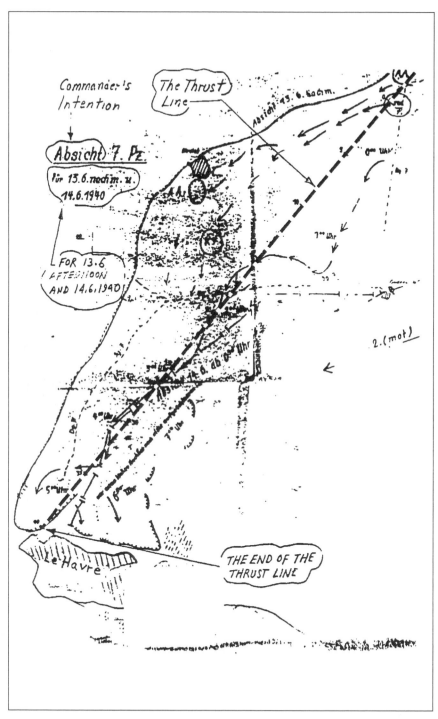

Figure 2. Example of a 7.Pz.D. Thrust Line, (13-14 June 1940).

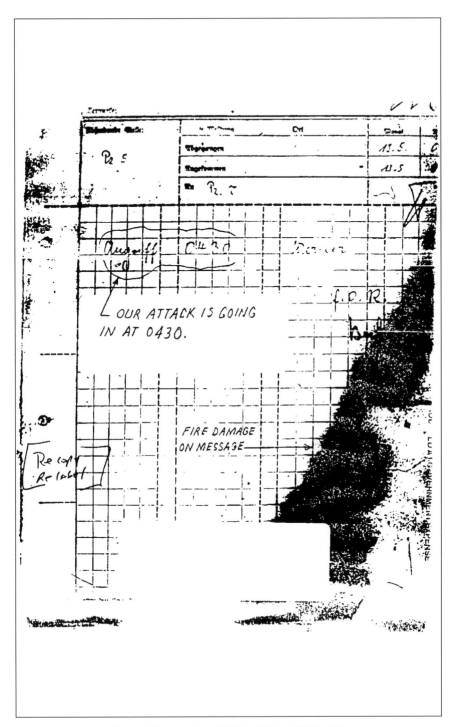

Figure 3. Message from 5.Pz.D. to 7.Pz.D., (13 May 40).

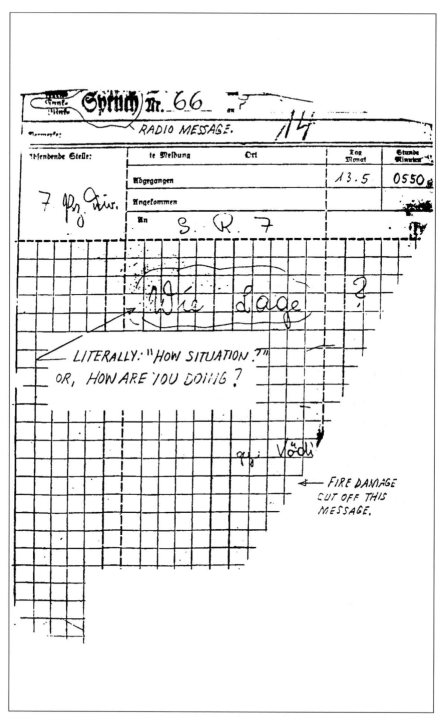

Figure 4. Message from 7.Pz.D. to S.R. 7, (13 May 40). Critical time 0550 in Meuse Crossing.

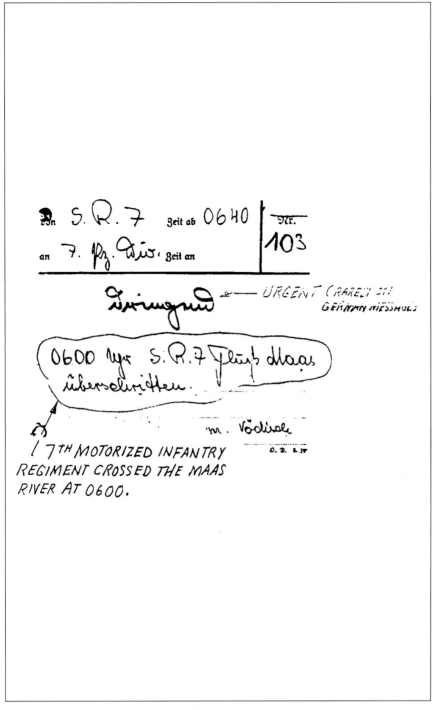

Figure 5. Message from S.R. 7 to 7.Pz.D., (13 May 40). Answer to division query of 0550.

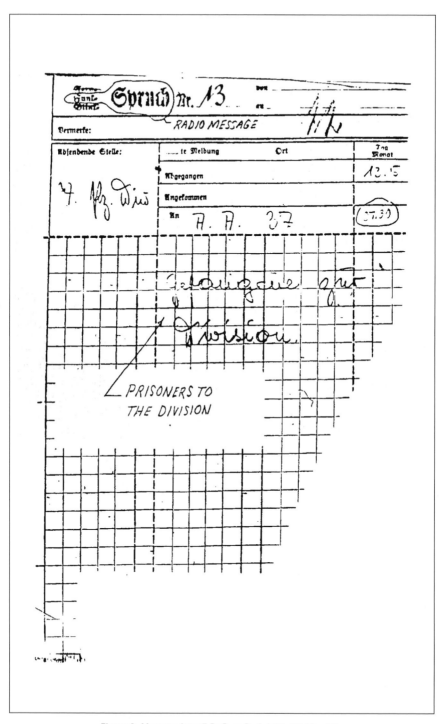

Figure 6. Message from 7.Pz.D. to Pz.A.A.37, (13 May 40).

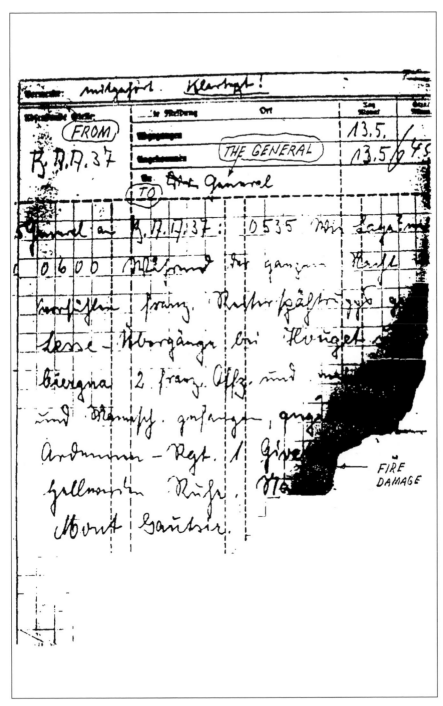

Figure 7. Note the style in the FROM/TO above.
The Commander of Pz.A.A.37 speaks directly to "The General" (Rommel), (13 May 40).

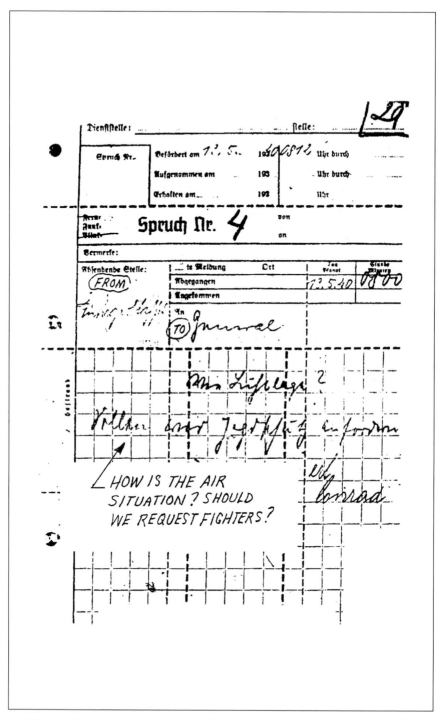

Figure 8. Message from Operations Staff to the General i.e., Rommel personally, (13 May 40).

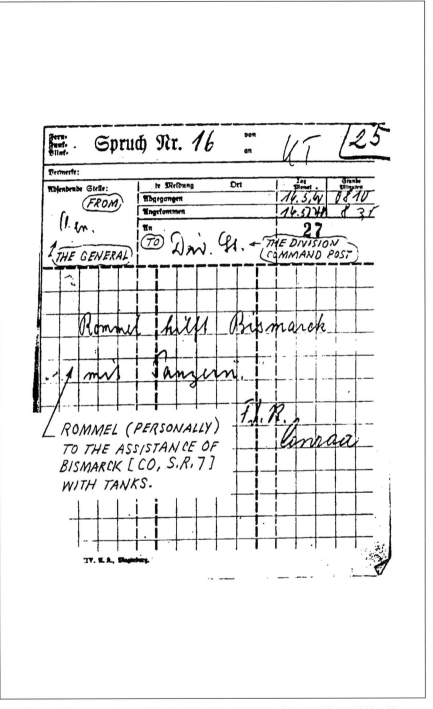

Figure 9. Message from the General personally to the Division Command Post, (14 May 40).

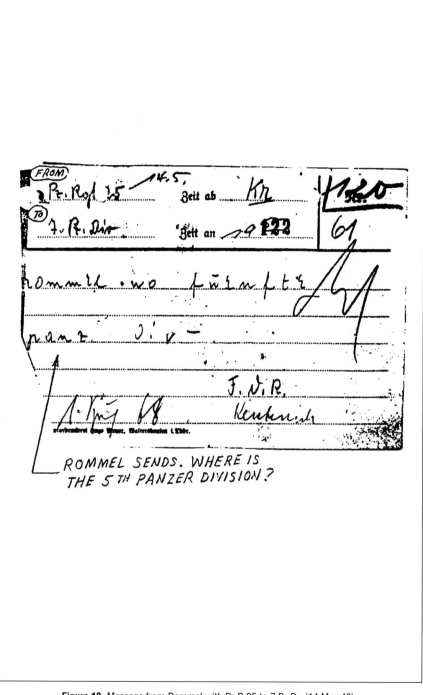

Figure 10. Message from Rommel with Pz.R.25 to 7.Pz.D., (14 May 40).

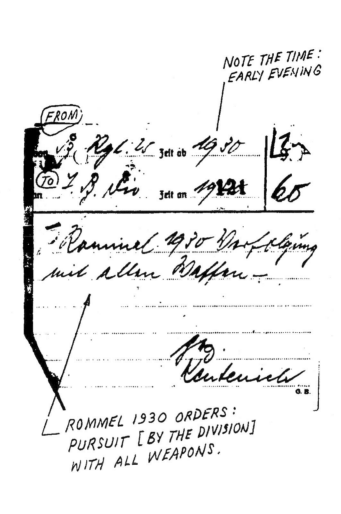

Figure 11. Message from Rommel with Pz.R.25 to 7.Pz.D., (14 May 40).

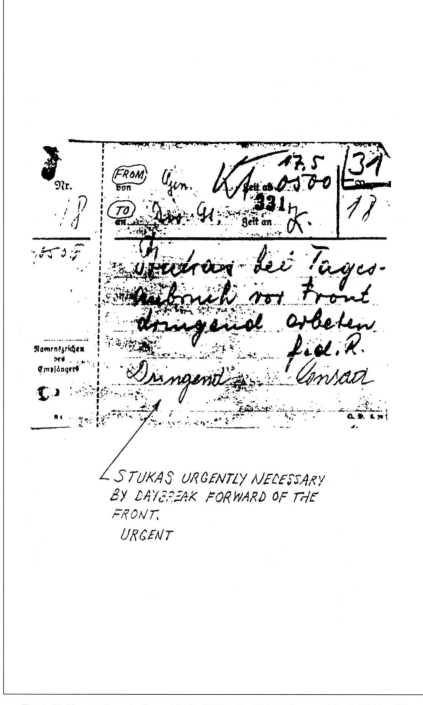

Figure 14. Message from the General (at Pz.R.25) to the Division Command Post, (17 May 40).

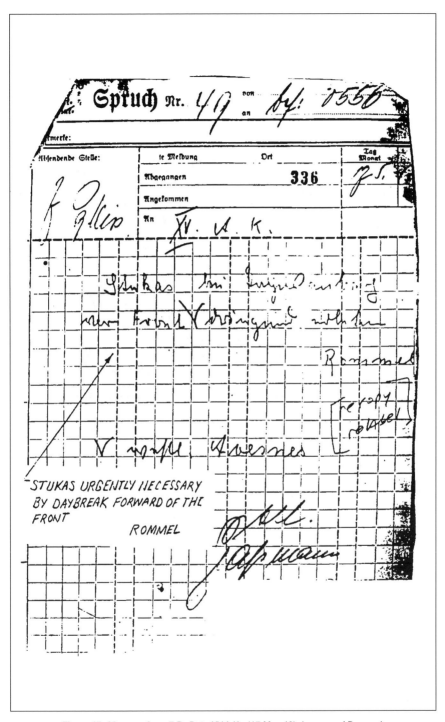

Figure 15. Message from 7.Pz.D. to XV.A.K., (17 May 40), in name of Rommel.

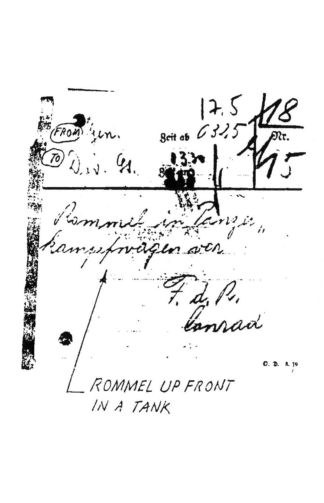

Figure 16. Message from the General to the Division Command Post, (17 May 40).

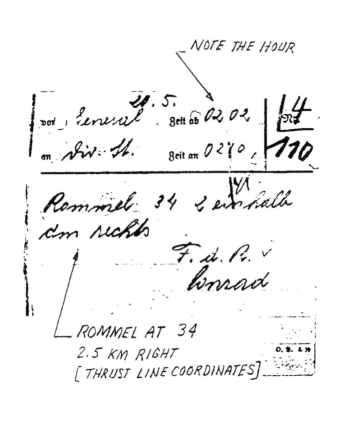

Figure 17. Message from the General to the Division Command Post immediately before the Night Attack, (19-20 May 40).

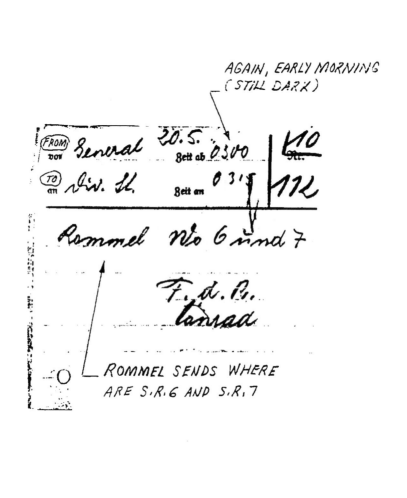

Figure 18. Message from the General to the Division Command Post, (20 May 40).

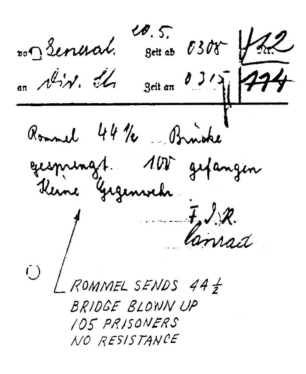

Figure 19. Message from the General to the Division Command Post, (20 May 40).

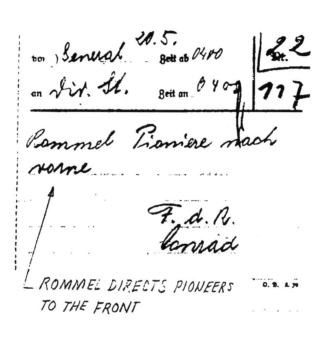

ROMMEL DIRECTS PIONEERS
TO THE FRONT

Figure 20. Message from the General to the Division Staff, (20 May 40) (Pioneers).

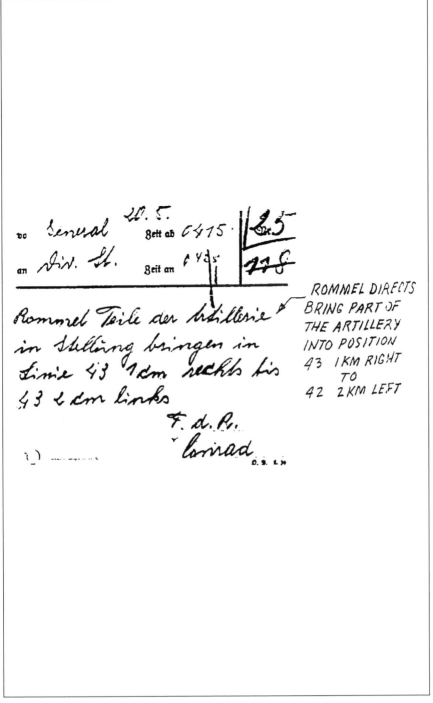

Figure 21. Message from the General to the Division Staff, (20 May 40) (Artillery).

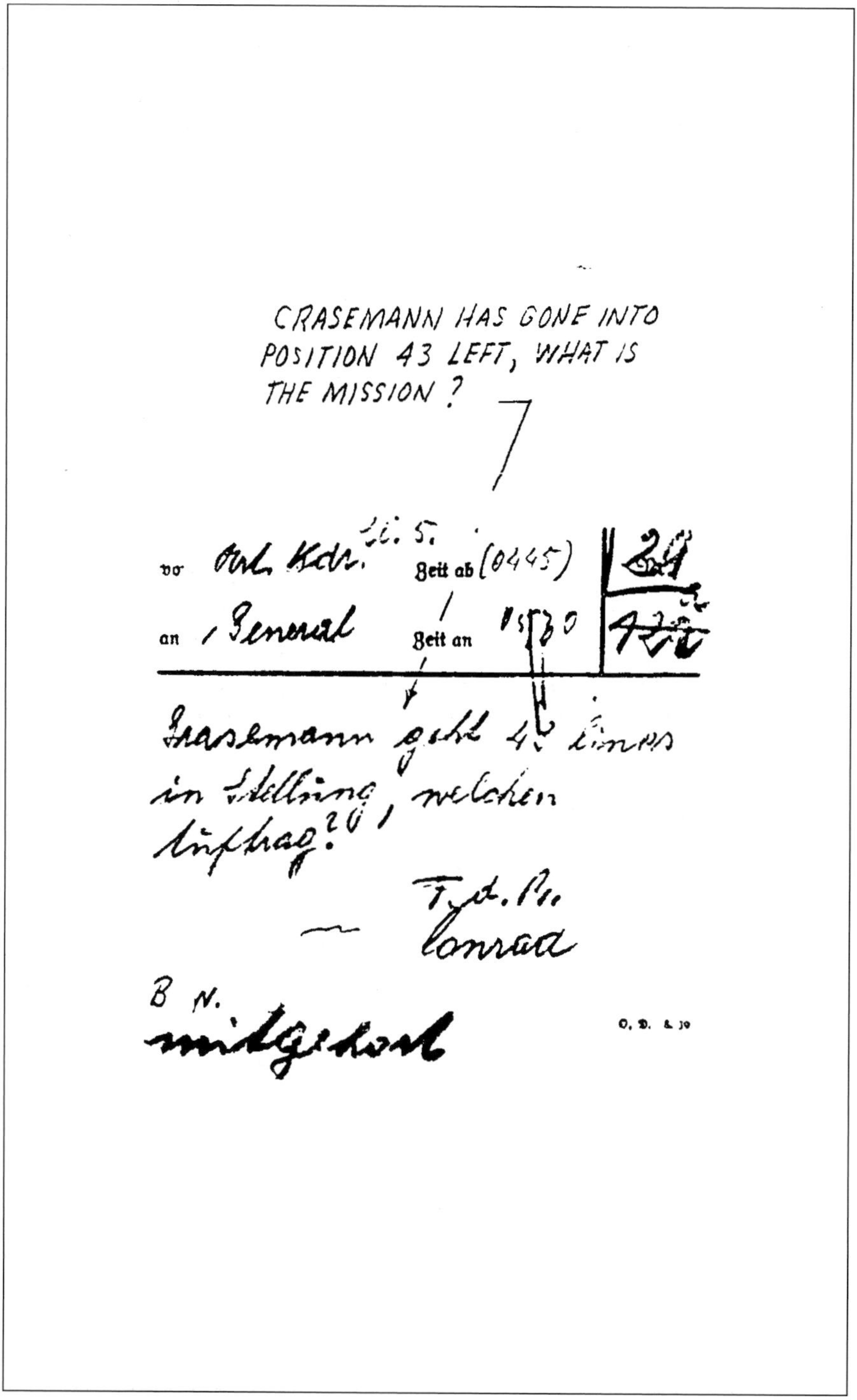

CRASEMANN HAS GONE INTO
POSITION 43 LEFT, WHAT IS
THE MISSION ?

Art. Kdr. *Li. 5.* Zeit ab (0445)

an / General Zeit an *1530*

Grasemann geht 43 links
in Stellung, welchen
Auftrag?

T.d.P.
Conrad

B N.
mitgedost

O. D. & 39

Figure 22. Message from the Artillery Commander to the General, (20 May 40) (Craseman).

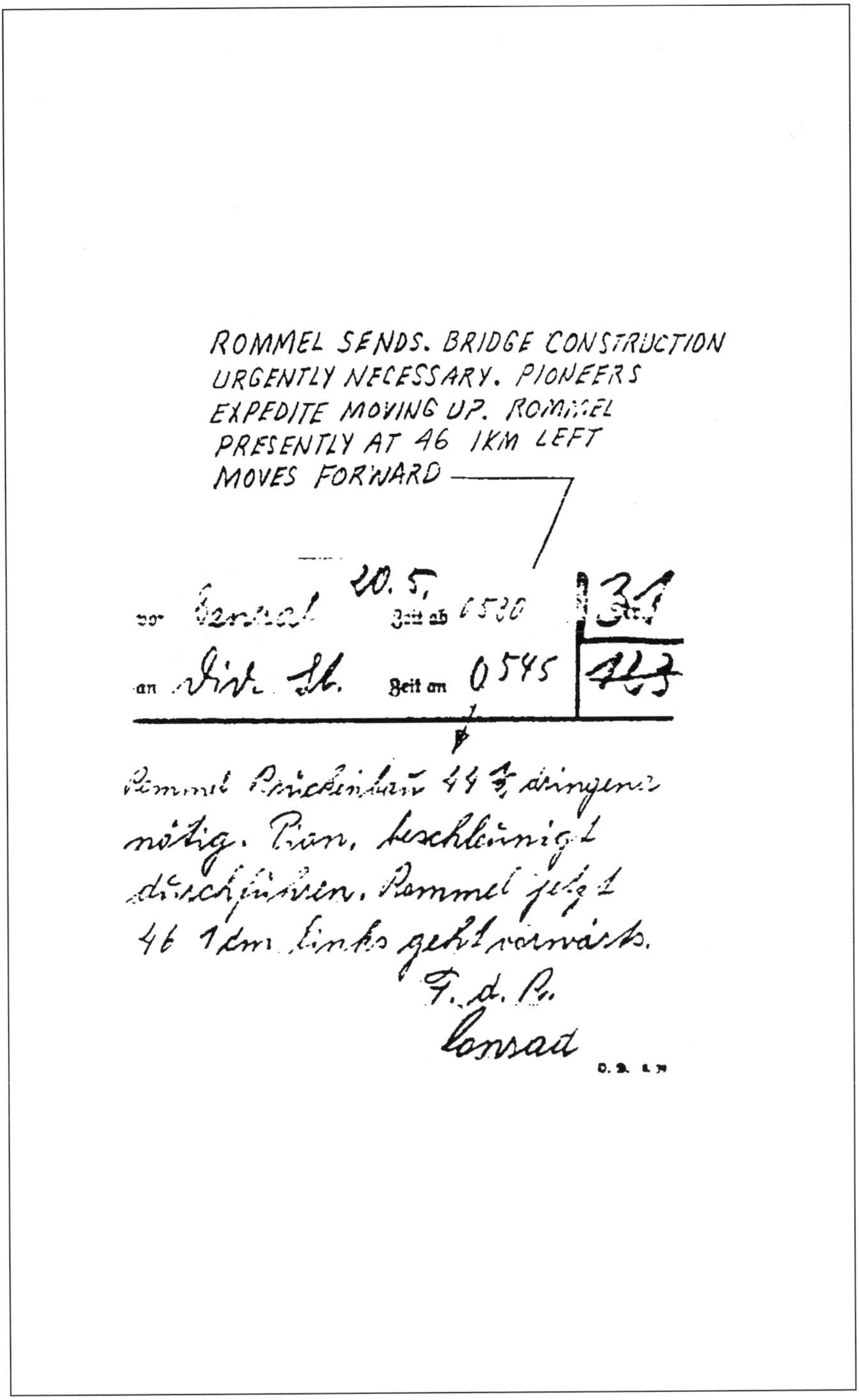

ROMMEL SENDS. BRIDGE CONSTRUCTION
URGENTLY NECESSARY. PIONEERS
EXPEDITE MOVING UP. ROMMEL
PRESENTLY AT 46 1KM LEFT
MOVES FORWARD

Figure 23. Message from the General to the Division Staff, (20 May 40) (Pioneers).

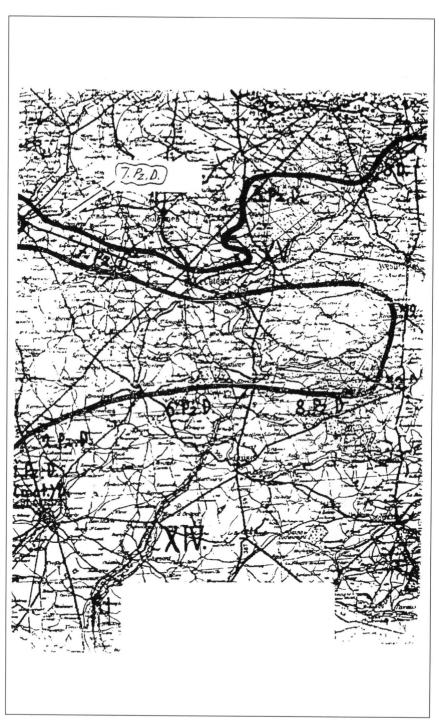

Map 2. Situation of 7.Pz.D. on evening of 18 May 40.

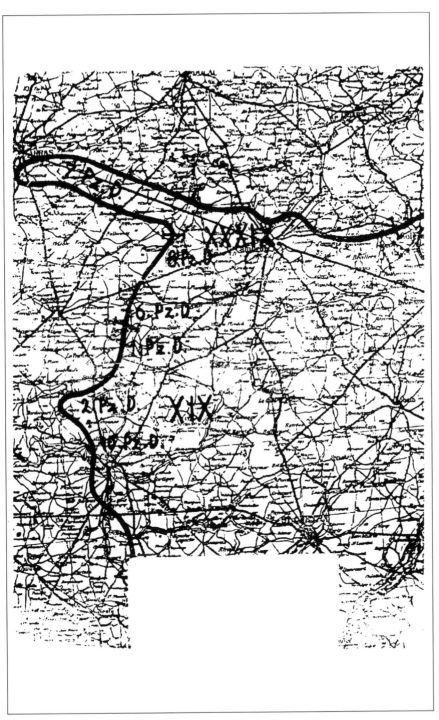

Map 3. Situation of 7.Pz.D. at approximately 0700, (20 May 40).

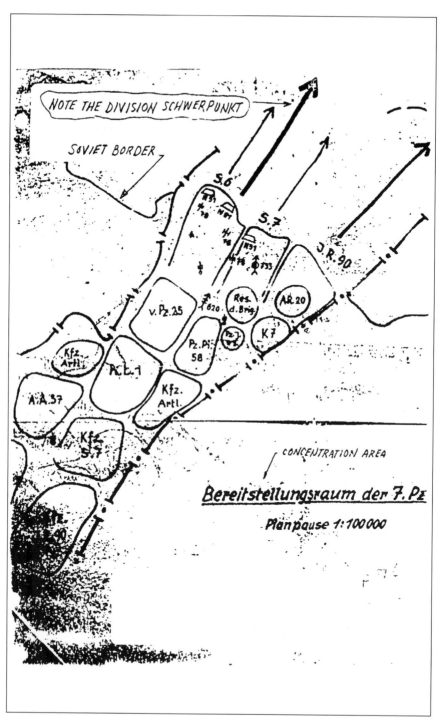

Map 4. Concentration Area of 7.Pz.D. for Attack on the Soviet Union, (22 June 41).

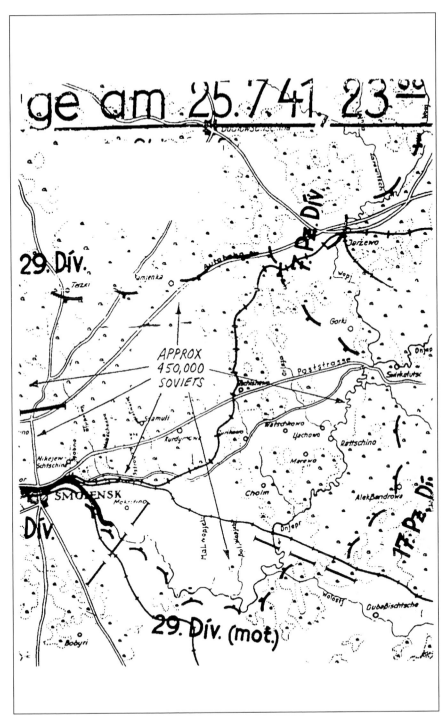

Map 7. Location of 7.Pz.D., (25 July 41).

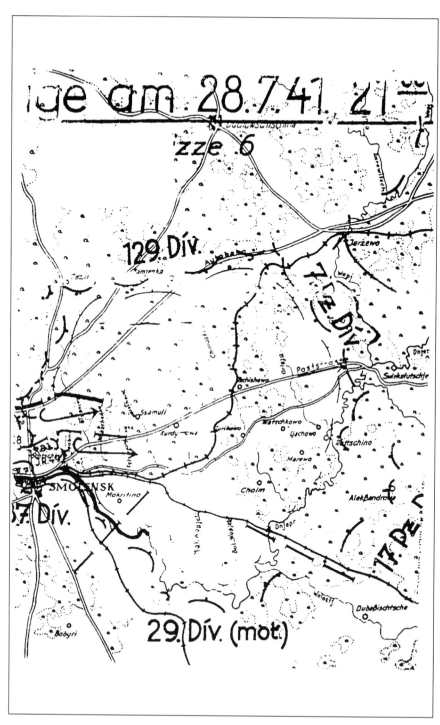

Map 8. Location of 7.Pz.D., (28 July 41).

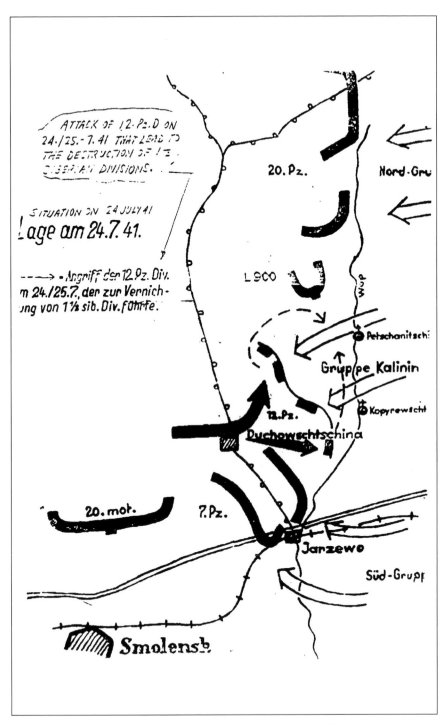

Map 9. Location of 7.Pz.D. and Attack of Soviet Group Kalinin, (24 July 41).